Harvard
Business
Review

ON

MANAGING YOUR CAREER

THE HARVARD BUSINESS REVIEW PAPERBACK SERIES

The series is designed to bring today's managers and professionals the fundamental information they need to stay competitive in a fast-moving world. From the preeminent thinkers whose work has defined an entire field to the rising stars who will redefine the way we think about business, here are the leading minds and landmark ideas that have established the *Harvard Business Review* as required reading for ambitious businesspeople in organizations around the globe.

Other books in the series:

Harvard Business Review Interviews with CEOs

Harvard Business Review on Advances in Strategy

Harvard Business Review on Becoming a High Performance Manager

Harvard Business Review on Brand Management

Harvard Business Review on Breakthrough Leadership

Harvard Business Review on Breakthrough Thinking

Harvard Business Review on Business and the Environment

Harvard Business Review on the Business Value of IT

Harvard Business Review on Change

Harvard Business Review on Compensation

Harvard Business Review on Corporate Governance

Harvard Business Review on Corporate Strategy

Harvard Business Review on Crisis Management

Harvard Business Review on Culture and Change

Harvard Business Review on Customer Relationship Management

Harvard Business Review on Decision Making

Harvard Business Review on Effective Communication

Harvard Business Review on Entrepreneurship

Harvard Business Review on Finding and Keeping the Best People

Harvard Business Review

ON

MANAGING YOUR CAREER

A HARVARD BUSINESS REVIEW PAPERBACK

The *Harvard Business Review* articles in this collection are available as
individual reprints. Discounts apply to quantity purchases. For information and ordering please contact Customer Service, Harvard Business
School Publishing, Boston, MA 02163. Telephone (617) 783-7500 or
(800) 988-0886, 8 A.M. to 6 P.M. Eastern Time, Monday through Friday.
Fax (617) 783-7555, 24 hours a day. E-mail: custserv@hbsp.harvard.edu

Library of Congress Cataloging-in-Publication Data
Harvard business review on managing your career.
      p.   cm. — (A Harvard business review paperback)
    Includes index.
    ISBN 1-59139-131-8 (alk. paper)
    1. Career development.   I. Harvard Business School Press.
II. Harvard business review.   III. Harvard business review paperback
series.
HF5381 .H278   2002
650.14—dc21   2002012681
                                                        CIP

*The paper used in this publication meets the requirements of the Ameri-
can National Standard for Permanence of Paper for Publications and
Documents in Libraries and Archives Z39.48-1992.*

Contents

Harvard Business Review

ON

MANAGING YOUR CAREER

Reawakening Your Passion for Work

RICHARD BOYATZIS, ANNIE MCKEE, AND
DANIEL GOLEMAN

Executive Summary

ALL OF US STRUGGLE from time to time with the question of personal meaning: "Am I living the way I want to live?" For millions of people, the attacks of September 11 put the issue front and center, but most of us periodically take stock of our lives under far less dramatic circumstances. This type of questioning is healthy; business leaders need to go through it every few years to replenish their energy, creativity, and commitment—and their passion for work.

In this article, the authors describe the signals that it's time to reevaluate your choices and illuminate strategies for responding to those signals. Such wake-up calls come in various forms. Some people feel trapped or bored and may realize that they have adjusted to the frustrations of their work to such an extent that they barely recognize themselves. For others, the signal comes when

1

they are faced with an ethical challenge or suddenly discover their true calling.

Once you have realized that it's time to take stock of your life, there are strategies to help you consider where you are, where you're headed, and where you want to be. Many people find that calling a time-out—either in the form of an intense, soul-searching exercise or a break from corporate life—is the best way to reconnect with their dreams. Other strategies include working with a coach, participating in an executive development program, scheduling regular time for self-reflection, and making small changes so that your work better reflects your values. People no longer expect their leaders to have all the answers, but they do expect them to try to keep their own passion alive and to support employees through that process.

LAST SEPTEMBER, as millions of people around the globe stared in disbelief at television screens, watching the World Trade Center towers crumble to the ground, many of us realized that accompanying the shock and sorrow was another sensation—the impulse to take stock. The fragile nature of human life, exposed with such unbearable clarity, compelled people to ask a haunting question: "Am I really living the way I want to live?"

We all struggle with the question of personal meaning throughout our lives. September 11, 2001, brought the issue into focus for many people all at once, but the impulse to take stock comes up periodically for most of us in far less dramatic circumstances. The senior executives who read this magazine, for instance, seem to struggle with this question at the high point of their careers. Why? Many executives hit their professional stride in their forties and fifties, just as their parents are reaching the end of their lives—a reminder that all of us are mortal. What's more, many of the personality traits associated with career success, such as a knack for problem solving and sheer tenacity, lead people to stick with a difficult situation in the hope of making it better. Then one day, a creeping sensation sets in: Something is wrong. That realization launches a process we have witnessed—literally thousands of times—in our work coaching managers and executives over the past 14 years.

The process is rarely easy, but we've found this type of awakening to be healthy and necessary; leaders need to go through it every few years to replenish their energy, creativity, and commitment—and to rediscover their passion for work and life. Indeed, leaders cannot keep achieving new goals and inspiring the people around them without understanding their own dreams. In this article, we'll look at the different signals that it's time to take stock—whether you have a nagging sense of doubt that builds over time until it's impossible to ignore or you experience a life-changing event that irrevocably alters your perspective. Then we'll describe some strategies for listening to those signals and taking restorative action. Such action can range from a relatively minor adjustment in outlook, to a larger refocusing on what really matters, to practical life changes that take you in an entirely new direction.

When to Say When

When asked, most businesspeople say that passion—to lead, to serve the customer, to support a cause or a product—is what drives them. When that passion fades, they begin to question the meaning of their work. How can you reawaken the passion and reconnect with what's meaningful for you? The first step is acknowledging the signal that it's time to take stock. Let's look at the various feelings that let you know the time has come.

"I FEEL TRAPPED."

Sometimes, a job that was fulfilling gradually becomes less meaningful, slowly eroding your enthusiasm and spirit until you no longer find much purpose in your work. People often describe this state as feeling trapped. They're restless, yet they can't seem to change—or even articulate what's wrong.

Take the case of Bob McDowell, the corporate director of human resources at a large professional-services firm. After pouring his heart and soul into his work for 25 years, Bob had become terribly demoralized because his innovative programs were cut time and again. As a result, his efforts could do little to improve the workplace over the long term. For years he had quieted his nagging doubts, in part because an occasional success or a rare employee who flourished under his guidance provided deep, if temporary, satisfaction. Moreover, the job carried all the usual trappings of success—title, money, and perks. And, like most people in middle age, McDowell had financial responsibilities that made it risky to trade security for personal fulfillment. Factors such as these conspire to keep people trudging along, hoping things will get better. But clinging to security or trying to be a good corporate citizen can turn out to be a prison of your own making.

Many people confuse achieving day-to-day business goals with performing truly satisfying work.

"I'M BORED."

Many people confuse achieving day-to-day business goals with performing truly satisfying work, so they continue setting and achieving new goals—until it dawns on them that they are bored. People are often truly shaken by this revelation; they feel as if they have just emerged from a spiritual blackout. We saw this in Nick Mimken, the owner of a successful insurance agency, who increasingly felt that something was missing from his life. He joined a book group, hoping that intellectual stimulation would help him regain some enthusiasm, but it wasn't enough. The fact was, he had lost touch with his dreams and was going through the motions at work without experiencing any real satisfaction from the success of his business.

High achievers like Mimken may have trouble accepting that they're bored because it's often the generally positive traits of ambition and determination to succeed that obscure the need for fun. Some people may feel guilty about being restless when it looks like they have it all. Others may admit they aren't having fun but believe that's the price of success. As one manager said, "I work to live. I don't expect to find deep meaning at the office; I get that elsewhere." The problem? Like many, this man works more than 60 hours a week, leaving him little time to enjoy anything else.

"I'M NOT THE PERSON I WANT TO BE."

Some people gradually adjust to the letdowns, frustrations, and even boredom of their work until they surrender to a routine that's incompatible with who they are and what they truly want. Consider, for instance, John Lauer, an inspirational leader who took over as president of BFGoodrich and quickly captured the support of top executives with his insight into the company's challenges and opportunities, and his contagious passion for the business.

But after he'd been with the company about six years, we watched Lauer give a speech to a class of executive MBA students and saw that he had lost his spark. Over time, Lauer had fallen in step with a corporate culture that was focused on shareholder value in a way that was inconsistent with what he cared about. Not surprisingly, he left the company six months later, breaking from corporate life by joining his wife in her work with Hungarian relief organizations. He later admitted that he knew he wasn't himself by the end of his time at BFGoodrich, although he didn't quite know why.

How did Lauer stray from his core? First, the change was so gradual that he didn't notice that he was being absorbed into a culture that didn't fit him. Second, like many, he did what he felt he "should," going along with the bureaucracy and making minor concession after minor concession rather than following his heart. Finally, he exhibited a trait that is a hallmark of effective leaders: adaptability. At first, adapting to the corporate culture probably made Lauer feel more comfortable. But without strong self-awareness, people risk adapting to such an extent that they no longer recognize themselves.

"I WON'T COMPROMISE MY ETHICS."

The signal to take stock may come to people in the form of a challenge to what they feel is right. Such was the case for Niall FitzGerald, now the cochairman of Unilever, when he was asked to take a leadership role in South Africa, which was still operating under apartheid.

The offer was widely considered a feather in his cap and a positive sign about his future with Unilever. Until that time, FitzGerald had accepted nearly every assignment, but the South Africa opportunity stopped him in his tracks, posing a direct challenge to his principles. How could he, in good conscience, accept a job in a country whose political and practical environment he found reprehensible?

Or consider the case of a manager we'll call Rob. After working for several supportive and loyal bosses, he found himself reporting to an executive—we'll call him Martin—whose management style was in direct conflict with Rob's values. The man's abusive treatment of subordinates had derailed a number of promising careers, yet he was something of a legend in the company. To Rob's chagrin, the senior executive team admired Martin's performance and, frankly, felt that young managers benefited from a stint under his marine lieutenant–style leadership.

When you recognize that an experience is in conflict with your values, as FitzGerald and Rob did, you can at least make a conscious choice about how to respond. The problem is, people often miss this particular signal because they lose sight of their core values. Sometimes they separate their work from their personal lives to such an extent that they don't bring their values to the office. As a result, they may accept or even engage in behaviors they'd deem unacceptable at home. Other people find that their work *becomes* their life, and business goals take precedence over everything else. Many executives who genuinely value family above all still end up working 12-hour days, missing more and more family dinners as they pursue success at work. In these cases, people may not hear the wake-up call. Even if they do, they may sense that something isn't quite right but be unable to identify it—or do anything to change it.

"I CAN'T IGNORE THE CALL."

A wake-up call can come in the form of a mission: an irresistible force that compels people to step out, step up, and take on a challenge. It is as if they suddenly recognize what they are meant to do and cannot ignore it any longer.

Such a call is often spiritual, as in the case of the executive who, after examining his values and personal vision, decided to quit his job, become ordained, buy a building, and start a church—all at age 55. But a call can take other forms as well—to become a teacher, to work with disadvantaged children, or to make a difference to the people you encounter every day. Rebecca Yoon, who runs a dry-cleaning business, has come to consider it her mission to connect with her customers on a personal level. Her constant and sincere attention has created remarkable loyalty to her shop, even though the actual service she provides is identical to that delivered by hundreds of other dry cleaners in the city.

"LIFE IS TOO SHORT!"

Sometimes it takes a trauma, large or small, to jolt people into taking a hard look at their lives. Such an awakening may be the result of a heart attack, the loss of a loved one, or a world tragedy. It can also be the result of something less dramatic, like adjusting to an empty nest or celebrating a significant birthday. Priorities can become crystal clear at times like these, and things that seemed important weeks, days, or even minutes ago no longer matter.

For example, following a grueling and heroic escape from his office at One World Trade Center last September, John Paul DeVito of the May Davis Group stumbled into a church in tears, desperate to call his family. When a police officer tried to calm him down, DeVito responded, "I'm not in shock. I've never been more cognizant in my life." Even as he mourned the deaths of friends and colleagues, he continued to be ecstatic about life, and he's now reframing his priorities, amazed that before this horrific experience he put duty to his job above almost everything else.

DeVito is not alone. Anecdotal evidence suggests that many people felt the need to seek new meaning in their lives after the tragedies of last September, which highlighted the fact that life can be cut short at any time. An article in the December 26, 2001, *Wall Street Journal* described two women who made dramatic changes after the attacks. Following a visit to New York shortly after the towers were hit, engineer Betty Roberts quit her job at age 52 to enroll in divinity school.

The quieter signals—a sense of unease that builds over time, for example—can be easy to miss or dismiss.

And Chicki Wentworth decided to give up the office and restaurant building she had owned and managed for nearly 30 years in order to work with troubled teens.

But as we've said, people also confront awakening events throughout their lives in much more mundane circumstances. Turning 40, getting married, sending a child to college, undergoing surgery, facing retirement—these are just a handful of the moments in life when we naturally pause, consider where our choices have taken us, and check our accomplishments against our dreams.

Interestingly, it's somehow more socially acceptable to respond to shocking or traumatic events than to any of the others. As a result, people who feel trapped and bored often stick with a job that's making them miserable for far too long, and thus they may be more susceptible to stress-related illnesses. What's more, the quieter signals—a sense of unease that builds over time, for example—can be easy to miss or dismiss because their day-to-day impact is incremental. But such signals are no less important as indicators of the need to reassess than the more visible events. How do you learn to listen to vital signals and respond before it's too late? It takes a conscious, disciplined effort at periodic self-examination.

Strategies for Renewal

There's no one-size-fits-all solution for restoring meaning and passion to your life. However, there are strategies for assessing your life and making corrections if you've gotten off course. Most people pursue not a single strategy but a combination, and some seek outside help while others prefer a more solitary journey. Regardless of which path you choose, you need time for reflection—a chance to consider where you are, where you're going, and where you really want to be. Let's look at five approaches.

CALL A TIME-OUT

For some people, taking time off is the best way to figure out what they really want to do and to reconnect with their dreams. Academic institutions have long provided time for rejuvenation through sabbaticals—six to 12 months off, often with pay. Some businesses—to be clear, very few—offer sabbaticals as well, letting people take a paid leave to pursue their interests with the guarantee of a job when they return. More often, business-people who take time off do so on their own time—a risk, to be sure, but few who have stepped off the track regret the decision.

This is the path Bob McDowell took. McDowell, the HR director we described earlier who felt trapped in his job, stepped down from his position, did not look for another job, and spent about eight months taking stock of his life. He considered his successes and failures, and faced up to the sacrifices he had made by dedicating himself so completely to a job that was, in the end, less than fulfilling. Other executives take time off with far less ambitious goals—simply to get their heads out of their work for a while and focus on their personal lives. After a time, they may very happily go back to the work they'd been doing for years, eager to embrace the same challenges with renewed passion.

Still others might want to step off the fast track and give their minds a rest by doing something different. When Nick Mimken, the bored head of an insurance agency, took stock of his life and finally realized he wasn't inspired by his work, he decided to sell his business, keep only a few clients, and take sculpture classes. He then went to work as a day laborer for a landscaper in order to pursue his interest in outdoor sculpture—in particular, stone fountains. Today he and his wife live in Nantucket, Massachusetts, where he no longer works *for* a living but *at* living. He is exploring what speaks to him—be it rock sculpture, bronze casting, protecting wildlife, or teaching people how to handle their money. Nick is deeply passionate about his work and how he is living his life. He calls himself a life explorer.

In any event, whether it's an intense, soul-searching exercise or simply a break from corporate life, people almost invariably find time-outs energizing. But stepping out isn't easy. No to-do list, no meetings or phone calls, no structure—it can be difficult for high achievers to abandon their routines. The loss of financial security makes this move inconceivable for some. And for the many people whose identities are tied up in their professional lives, walking away feels like too great a sacrifice. Indeed, we've seen people jump back onto the train within a week or two without reaping any benefit from the time off, just because they could not stand to be away from work.

FIND A PROGRAM

While a time-out can be little more than a refreshing pause, a leadership or executive development program is a more structured strategy, guiding people as they explore their dreams and open new doors.

Remember John Lauer? Two years after Lauer left BFGoodrich, he was still working with Hungarian refugees (his time-out) and maintained that he wanted nothing to do with running a company. Yet as part of his search for the next phase of his career, he decided to pursue an executive doctorate degree. While in the program, he took a leadership development seminar in which a series of exercises forced him to clarify his values, philosophy, aspirations, and strengths. (See "Tools for Reflection" at the end of this article to learn more about some of these exercises.)

In considering the next decade of his life and reflecting on his capabilities, Lauer realized that his resistance to running a company actually represented a fear of replicating his experience at BFGoodrich. In fact, he loved being at the helm of an organization where he could convey his vision and lead the company forward, and he relished working with a team of like-minded executives. Suddenly, he realized that he missed those aspects of the CEO job and that in the right kind of situation—one in which he could apply the ideas he'd developed in his studies—being a CEO could be fun.

With this renewed passion to lead, Lauer returned a few headhunters' calls and within a month was offered the job of chairman and CEO at Oglebay Norton, a $250 million company in the raw-materials business. There he became an exemplar of the democratic leadership style, welcoming employees' input and encouraging his leadership team to do the same. As one of his executives told us, "John raises our spirits, our confidence, and our passion for excellence." Although the company deals in such unglamorous commodities as gravel and sand, Lauer made so many improvements in his first year that Oglebay Norton was featured in *Fortune, BusinessWeek,* and the *Wall Street Journal.*

Another executive we know, Tim Schramko, had a long career managing health care companies. As a diversion, he began teaching part-time. He took on a growing course load while fulfilling his business responsibilities, but he was running himself ragged. It wasn't until he went through a structured process to help him design his ideal future that he realized he had a calling to teach. Once that was clear, he developed a plan for extricating himself from his business obligations over a two-year period and is now a full-time faculty member.

Many educational institutions offer programs that support this type of move. What's more, some companies have developed their own programs in the realization that leaders who have a chance to reconnect with their dreams tend to return with redoubled energy and commitment. The risk, of course, is that after serious reflection, participants will jump ship. But in our experience, most find new meaning and passion in their current positions. In any event, people who do leave weren't in the right job—and they would have realized it sooner or later.

CREATE "REFLECTIVE STRUCTURES"

When leadership guru Warren Bennis interviewed leaders from all walks of life in the early 1990s, he found that they had a common way of staying in touch with what was important to them. They built into their lives what Bennis calls "reflective structures," time and space for self-examination, whether a few hours a week, a day or two a month, or a longer period every year.

For many people, religious practices provide an outlet for reflection, and some people build time into the day or week for prayer or meditation. But reflection does not have to involve organized religion. Exercise is an outlet for many people, and some executives set aside time in their calendars for regular workouts. One CEO of a $2 billion utility company reserves eight hours a week for solitary reflection—an hour a day, perhaps two or three hours on a weekend. During that time, he might go for a long walk, work in his home shop, or take a ride on his Harley. However you spend the time, the idea is to get away from the demands of your job and be with your own thoughts.

Increasingly, we've seen people seek opportunities for collective reflection as well, so that they can share their dreams and frustrations with their peers. On his third time heading a major division of the Hay Group, Murray

Dalziel decided to build some reflection into his life by joining a CEO group that meets once a month. In a sense, the group legitimizes time spent thinking, talking, and learning from one another. Members have created a trusting community where they can share honest feedback—a scarce resource for most executives. And all gain tangible benefits; people exchange tips on how to fix broken processes or navigate sticky situations.

WORK WITH A COACH

Our own biases and experiences sometimes make it impossible for us to find a way out of a difficult or confusing situation; we need an outside perspective. Help can come informally from family, friends, and colleagues, or it can come from a professional coach skilled at helping people see their strengths and identify new ways to use them. We won't discuss more traditional therapy in this article, but it is, of course, another alternative.

When Bob McDowell, the HR director, stepped out of his career, he sought out a variety of personal and professional connections to help him decide how to approach the future. Working with an executive coach, McDowell was able to identify what was important to him in life and translate that to what he found essential in a job. He could then draw clear lines around the aspects of his personal life he would no longer compromise, including health and exercise, time with his family, personal hobbies, and other interests. In the end, he found his way to a new career as a partner in an executive search business—a job he'd never considered but one that matched his passion for helping people and the companies they work for. What's more, his soul-searching had so sparked his creativity that in his new position he combined traditional organizational consulting with the search process to discover unusual possibilities. Instead of a typical executive search, he helps companies find employees who will bring magic to the business and to the relationships essential to success.

What did the coach bring to McDowell's self-reflection? Perhaps the chief benefit was a trusting, confidential relationship that gave him the space to dream—something executives shy away from, largely because the expectations of society and their families weigh on them so heavily. Like many, McDowell began this process assuming that he would simply narrow his priorities, clarify his work goals, and chart a new professional path. But to his surprise, his coach's perspective helped him see new opportunities in every part of his life, not just in his work.

Sometimes, however, the coach does little more than help you recognize what you already know at some level. Richard Whiteley, the cofounder of a successful international consulting firm and author of several business best-sellers, felt that he wasn't having as much fun as he used to; he was restless and wanted a change. To that end, he began to do some work on the side, helping businesspeople improve their effectiveness through spiritual development. He was considering leaving his consulting practice behind altogether and concentrating on the spiritual work—but he was torn. He turned to a spiritual leader, who told him, "Forget the spiritual work and concentrate on the work you've been doing." Only when forced to choose the wrong path could Richard recognize what he truly wanted to do. Within a few months, Richard had devoted himself to writing and speaking almost exclusively on spirituality and passion in work—and he's thriving.

FIND NEW MEANING IN FAMILIAR TERRITORY

It's not always feasible to change your job or move somewhere new, even if your situation is undesirable. And frankly, many people don't want to make such major changes. But it is often easier than you might think to make small adjustments so that your work more directly reflects your beliefs and values—as long as you know what you need and have the courage to take some risks.

Back to Niall FitzGerald, who was confronted with the decision over whether to live and work in South Africa. A strong and principled person as well as a good corporate citizen, FitzGerald eventually decided to break with company culture by accepting the job on one unprecedented condition: If over the first six months or so he found his involvement with the country intolerable, he would be allowed to take another job at Unilever, no questions asked. He then set forth to find ways to exert a positive influence on his new work environment wherever possible.

As the leader of a prominent business, FitzGerald had some clout, of course, but he knew that he could not take on the government directly. His response: Figure out what he *could* change, do it, and then deal with the system. For example, when he was building a new plant, the architect showed FitzGerald plans with eight bathrooms—four each for men and women, segregated by the four primary racial groups, as mandated by law. Together, the eight bathrooms would consume one-quarter of an entire floor.

FitzGerald rejected the plans, announcing that he would build two bathrooms, one for men and one for women, to the highest possible standards. Once the plant was built, government officials inspected the building, noticed the discrepancy, and asked him what he planned to do about it. He responded, "They're not segregated because we chose not to do so. We don't agree with segregation. These are very fine toilets . . . you could have your lunch on the floor. . . . I don't have a problem at all. You have a problem, and you have to decide what you are going to do. I'm doing nothing." The government did not respond immediately, but later the law was quietly changed. FitzGerald's act of rebellion was small, but it was consistent with his values and was the only stand he could have taken in good conscience. Living one's values in this way, in the face of opposition, is energizing. Bringing about change that can make a difference to the people around us gives meaning to our work, and for many people, it leads to a renewed commitment to their jobs.

For Rob, the manager who found himself reporting to an abusive boss, the first step was to look inward and admit that every day would be a challenge. By becoming very clear about his own core values, he could decide moment to moment how to deal with Martin's demands. He could determine whether a particular emotional reaction was a visceral response to a man he didn't respect or a reaction to a bad idea that he would need to confront. He could choose whether to do what he thought was right or to collude with what felt wrong. His clarity allowed him to stay calm and focused, do his job well, and take care of the business and the people around him. In the end, Rob came out of a difficult situation knowing he had kept his integrity without compromising his career, and in that time, he even learned and grew professionally. He still uses the barometer he developed during his years with Martin to check actions and decisions against his values, even though his circumstances have changed.

Another executive we've worked with, Bart Morrison, ran a nonprofit organization for ten years and was widely considered a success by donors, program recipients, and policy makers alike. Yet he felt restless and wondered if a turn as a company executive—which would mean higher compensation—would satisfy his urge for a new challenge. Morrison didn't really need more money, although it would have been a plus, and he had a deep sense of social mission and commitment to his work. He also acknowledged that working in the private sector would not realistically offer him any meaningful new challenges. In our work together, he brainstormed about different avenues he could take while continuing in the nonprofit field, and it occurred to him that he could write books and give speeches. These new activities gave him the excitement he had been looking for and allowed him to stay true to his calling.

It's worth noting that executives often feel threatened when employees start asking, "Am I doing what I want to do with my life?" The risk is very real that the answer will be no, and companies can lose great contributors. The impulse, then, may be to try to suppress such exploration. Many executives also avoid listening to their own signals, fearing that a close look at their dreams and aspirations will reveal severe disappointments, that to be true to themselves they will have to leave their jobs and sacrifice everything they have worked so hard to achieve.

But although people no longer expect leaders to have all the answers, they do expect their leaders to be open to the questions—to try to keep their own passion alive and to support employees through the same process. After all, sooner or later most people will feel an urgent need to take stock—and if they are given the chance to heed the call, they will most likely emerge stronger, wiser, and more determined than ever.

Tools for Reflection

ONCE YOU'VE LOST TOUCH with your passion and dreams, the very routine of work and the habits of your mind can make it difficult to reconnect. Here are some tools that can help people break from those routines and allow their dreams to come to the surface again.

Reflecting on the Past

Alone and with trusted friends and advisers, periodically do a reality check. Take an hour or two and draw your "lifeline." Beginning with childhood, plot the high points and the low points—the events that caused you great joy and great sorrow. Note the times you were most proud, most excited, and most strong and clear. Note also the times you felt lost and alone. Point out for yourself the transitions—times when things fundamentally changed for you. Now, look at the whole. What are some of the underlying themes? What seems to be ever present, no matter the situation? What values seem to weigh in most often and most heavily when you make changes in your life? Are you generally on a positive track, or have there been lots of ups and downs? Where does luck or fate fit in?

Now, switch to the more recent past and consider these questions: What has or has not changed at work, in life? How am I feeling? How do I see myself these days? Am I living my values? Am I having fun? Do my values still fit with what I need to do at work and with what my company is doing? Have my dreams changed? Do I still believe in my vision of my future?

As a way to pull it all together, do a bit of free-form writing, finishing the sentence, "In my life I . . . and now I. . . ."

Defining Your Principles for Life

Think about the different aspects of your life that are important, such as family, relationships, work, spirituality, and physical health. What are your core values in each of those areas? List five or six principles that guide you in life and think about whether they are values that you truly live by or simply talk about.

Extending the Horizon

Try writing a page or two about what you would like to do with the rest of your life. Or you might want to number a sheet of paper 1 through 27 and then list all the things you want to do or experience before you die. Don't feel the need to stop at 27, and don't worry about priorities or practicality—just write down whatever comes to you.

This exercise is harder than it seems because it's human nature to think more in terms of what we have to do—by tomorrow, next week, or next month. But with such a short horizon, we can focus only on what's urgent, not on what's important. When we think in terms of the extended horizon, such as what we might do before we die, we open up a new range of possibilities. In our work with leaders who perform this exercise, we've seen a surprising trend: Most people jot down a few career goals, but 80% or more of their lists have nothing to do with work. When they finish the exercise and study their writing, they see patterns that help them begin to crystallize their dreams and aspirations.

Envisioning the Future

Think about where you would be sitting and reading this article if it were 15 years from now and you were living your ideal life. What kinds of people would be around you? How would your environment look and feel? What might you be doing during a typical day or week? Don't worry about the feasibility of creating this life; rather, let the image develop and place yourself in the picture.

Try doing some free-form writing about this vision of yourself, speak your vision into a tape recorder, or talk about it with a trusted friend. Many people report that, when doing this exercise, they experience a release of energy and feel more optimistic than they had even moments earlier. Envisioning an ideal future can be a powerful way to connect with the possibilities for change in our lives.

Originally published in April 2002
Reprint R0204G

Goodbye Career, Hello Success

RANDY KOMISAR

Executive Summary

LIKE EVERY OTHER AMBITIOUS, Ivy League-educated baby boomer, Randy Komisar wanted to climb the corporate ladder—any corporate ladder. But he just couldn't bring himself to play the traditional career game. Instead, Komisar made up his own rules, taking a series of jobs that sparked his passions and made him happy—and successful.

Today, the charismatic 45-year-old is a "virtual CEO"—an off-site but super-charged consultant to flesh-and-blood CEOs at a number of start-up companies in Silicon Valley and beyond. But that was only after he'd worked his way through 11 companies in 25 years—a crazy quilt of jobs as a music promoter, corporate lawyer, CFO at a software start-up, and chief executive at a video game company, just to name a few.

Komisar's success came by *not* having a career—at least, not in the traditional old-economy sense of the word. He realized there were alternatives to marching your way straight up the corporate ladder and that success in the new economy can involve a series of twists and turns. In this first-person account, Komisar describes why a nontraditional career path such as the one he unintentionally took may appeal to more businesspeople than might suspect it themselves. He tracks his professional journey along a sometimes tense, often enlightening, and ultimately prosperous course. He shares lessons learned along the way.

Komisar also makes a strong business case for pursuing the passion-driven career; such a career, he says, makes supreme sense in the new economy because it's flexible and challenging—both for an individual and for the companies he chooses to work for.

B Y CONVENTIONAL STANDARDS, my résumé is a disaster. Eleven companies in 25 years, not to mention a crazy quilt of jobs: community development manager, music promoter, corporate lawyer, CFO at a technology start-up, and chief executive at a video game company, just to name a few. I zigged, then I zagged, then I zigged some more. By my résumé alone, no one should hire me.

Like every other ambitious, Ivy League–educated baby boomer, I set out to have a career. I tried, I really did. But I just couldn't.

Except that these days, plenty of companies would. And they do. At last, my "noncareer" career makes perfect sense—to them and to me.

Right now, I'm a "virtual CEO." That's a job title that was cooked up for my business card two years ago to describe my latest incarnation. I work with flesh-and-blood CEOs, mainly of Silicon Valley start-ups, to set strategy, raise money, and put a dynamic organization together very quickly. I work with five or six companies at a time, and I'm paid largely with equity. That way, everyone can be sure that I'm earning my keep. So far, being a virtual CEO has been a blast—fun, exciting, interesting. Everything you could want in a job.

But how did I get here? By not having a career. Now, that wasn't intentional. Like every other ambitious, Ivy League–educated baby boomer, I set out to have a career. I longed to impress friends, relatives, and former roommates with my titles and authority. I craved the chance to march up a corporate ladder—any corporate ladder at all. And I tried, I really did. But I just couldn't. My whole life, I have been constitutionally unable to play the career game by its rules. So I ended up following another route: taking jobs that, one after another, made me happy. Jobs that sparked my passion. What a lucky accident that was.

While it was in full throttle, my career made no sense looking through the windshield of the car. In fact, for many years, I couldn't fully explain my professional path to anyone, especially not my family. But today, looking in the rearview mirror, my career makes enormous sense. After all, it ultimately landed me in *my* perfect job. Sometimes I feel as if I couldn't have become a virtual CEO any other way.

I'm not going to argue that a "career" like mine is for everyone. It's not, especially with its emotional and financial ups and downs—and its unnerving lack of a safety net. But a passion-driven career does have some major virtues that perhaps make it a good choice for more people than suspect it themselves. First, it's never dull. Scary, yes. Confounding, often. But boring, never. You're always learning about yourself, other people, business, and the world, and that feels terrific. It feels meaningful. Second, a passion-driven career is good for the companies you work for because you're there for the love of the work. You can feel some satisfaction from giving your all to an organization. Third, a passion-driven career, with all its fluidity and flexibility, actually happens to make supreme sense in the ever-changing landscape of the new economy. Conventional careers require that you put one foot in front of the other, steady as you go. First you get one kind of experience, then you get another. Inch by inch, you march forward. The noncareer career doesn't involve much marching. Instead, when opportunity calls, you leap. And when opportunity dries up, you move on. You also tango, roll around in the mud, and jump for joy. It all depends on where you have taken yourself.

But the best thing about a career like mine is that it isn't a career at all. It's a life. Several years ago, just when I thought my job history couldn't get any more unconventional, it dawned on me that I had to stop separating Randy Komisar into two boxes: work and personal. I realized that one person went to work, and one person came home and laughed or cried about how work felt. So, only one person had to make decisions about which jobs to take and which jobs to leave. There couldn't be a distinction anymore between my career and my happiness, or my career and my identity. They are all pieces of one life—my life.

When you lump together career goals and personal goals to get life, you are certain to find at first that day-to-day existence is more confusing. It's definitely easier to compartmentalize, to do whatever it takes to get the money at work and make excuses later to your family and friends. "After all, it's only business. I'm not really like that," you say. But over time, I've also discovered that when you stop distinguishing between work life and personal life, you stop caring about a lot of things that used to seem so important—like the title on your business card. At the beginning, that feels frightening—and humbling, too. But it also feels authentic. Better yet, it feels sustainable. I'm 45 now, and I feel as if, finally, I don't have to survive solely on adrenaline, speed, and agility. I can just follow one passion—one job—to the next and call it life.

Father's Footsteps

My career started out just as it was supposed to. I was a young overachiever. I grew up in a comfortable suburb of Rochester, New York, where I excelled in school and participated in all the right extracurricular activities. Right on schedule, I got into Brown University. After that, I figured, all I needed was a great job, and I would be on my way to career fame and fortune.

But there was one distinct impediment to my plan, and it was buried in my genes. My father was not what you would call a career man. He never seemed to be at the same job very long. He owned a restaurant, a used-car lot, a gas station. He was an independent sales rep for paint, lighting fixtures, and jewelry. He started many little ventures, met early success, got tired of each, and left them to wither. Between those endeavors, he would sell anything he could get his hands on: water purifiers, burglar alarms, even Nigerian dried fish.

My father was also, let's say, an avid gambler. The casinos thought enough of him to regularly fly him into their clutches, and when he wasn't in Las Vegas or Atlantic City, he would find a good game of poker in town. Risk taking was in his blood. Now, I realize that it is also in mine—although it has played itself out in very different ways. I like to gamble, but not with money. I like to gamble with ideas, as many at a time as is humanly possible. I like to pour energy into them and see if they'll ignite.

Even though I entered Brown with dreams of a high-powered career in something—anything—the school itself did little to send me on my way. I mean that as a compliment. With few required courses, the opportunity to invent your own majors, and a pass-fail option throughout, Brown left me to navigate my own education. I quickly realized that other students were my best teachers. I fell into an eclectic group of free thinkers who, after a day of classes, sat around into the wee hours discussing their passions: union organizing, human rights, theater, writing, music, filmmaking. By graduation, I had been exposed to dozens of ideas and occupations, any one of which could have taken me a lifetime to pursue. I was intrigued by them all.

I was an economics major, and, for a while, I considered a career in the field but wasn't exactly sure what that would entail. I was on the verge of dedicating my senior year to earning a master's degree in economics when at the last minute I became excited by something old, literature, and something new, computers. Forget the master's degree, I decided. There were other interesting worlds out there to investigate.

Upon my graduation in 1976, I had no idea what to do next. I applied to Harvard Business School, which had the good sense to reject me. I then applied to big banks and advertising agencies, mostly in New York. I didn't know a thing about either type of business, but from 10,000 feet they looked interesting. Chemical Bank took the bait and called me in for interviews. But officials there quickly realized what soon became clear to me as well: I was not a banker. The ad agencies saved themselves the trouble and didn't respond to me at all.

I thought IBM might be interested in me because I had taken a computer course in my senior year and was well versed in punch cards—quite an unusual skill at the time for someone other than an engineer. I applied at the company's Providence, Rhode Island, office and took some kind of personality tests in the morning before my afternoon interviews. When I returned from lunch, the results were in, and they politely, but firmly, informed me that an interview would not be necessary. My high-powered career wasn't off to a promising start, but I wasn't worried. I just needed to find the right jumping-off point, I figured, and the race would begin.

Then, one summer day, long after most Brown students were off to their jobs as White House interns or astronauts in training, I spotted a small notice on a bulletin board in the placement office. It advertised a job in the planning department of the Providence Mayor's Office of Community Development. One interview later, I was smitten with the prospect of working to improve the city. I would be doing some economic analysis, working with a nice group, and helping poor people get a fair break with housing. Plus, the pay was okay, and the job came with a desk. I took it.

The city hall gig was fascinating, but it didn't fulfill my passion for business—for making deals. Not that I knew that deal making was one of my passions at the time. (Who used the word "deal" in 1976?) I soon found a second job to fill my nights and weekends. I attached myself to the Banzini Brothers, a small operation that staged rock concerts and other performances in the area

As far as I could tell, real careers involved a great deal of pain and angst.

between Boston and New York. In short order, I learned that there actually were jobs where people made money while thoroughly enjoying themselves. You have to remember, these were the days of sex, drugs, and rock and roll.

Crazy as it may sound, my two jobs didn't satisfy me completely. I had an idea that teaching might be an interesting career direction. So, in this same period, I became an economics instructor at Johnson & Wales College, a small liberal arts school in Providence. There, I taught one evening class per term, mainly to returning Vietnam veterans.

I kept at these three parallel "careers" for much of two years, and along the way I picked up knowledge that still guides me today. I learned about the byzantine politics of government organizations. I discovered what a roller coaster the entertainment business could be and realized that our cultural heroes could have childlike egos and one-dimensional personalities. And at Johnson & Wales, I saw that credentials could be bestowed for a price. Still, the polygamous nature of my professional life just didn't feel right. I knew none of my current jobs was going to pan out into the "big" career I had dreamed of. Plus, I wasn't suffering, and as far as I could tell from my college friends who had landed jobs with *Fortune* 500 companies and the like, real careers involved a great deal of pain and angst.

I decided I had to get serious. In 1978, I applied to Harvard Law School, convinced that my business intuition would substitute for an MBA. (Little did I know that the sum total of my business experience at the time actually amounted to the equivalent of running a lemon-ade stand.) The law, on the other hand, was something that I needed to crack; it appeared to me that lawyers were the real movers and shakers. They were the wise consiglieres at the mayor's office, the fixers for the Banzini Brothers, the real-estate developers in the com-munity development program, and the agents for the stars. Many of them impressed me with their structured, deductive thinking. All I needed was a good dose of that, and my career would be on its way.

At Harvard Law School, I threw myself into my studies. But even with my eyes fixed on the prize, I felt out of step. My peers roamed the campus in Brooks Brothers suits, scoring interviews at prestigious law firms. I couldn't bring myself to join the fray. The summer after my first year, I successfully avoided the huge salaries of private practice and found a work-study job in the San Francisco district attorney's office, prosecuting white-collar crime. My second summer, I deviated from the norm again and worked at the Federal Trade Commission.

During the school year, I made ends meet with a work-study stint at MassPIRG, Ralph Nader's public-interest research group in Massachusetts. The job injected a shot of passion into my otherwise sterile law school existence. And that gave me an idea: I could piece together the high-powered career I had dreamed about by working a dry, prestigious job during the day and by nurturing a rich, satisfying life of public-interest work—or whatever else excited me at the time—at night. Not perfect, I rea-soned, but close.

It was a boom time for private law firms, and they needed Harvard grads—even oddballs like me. I joined one of the biggest old-line firms in Boston.

My what-if scenario made even more sense when Ronald Reagan was elected president. My law school adviser pulled me aside soon afterward. "The money that funds public-interest law firms is going to dry up," he warned. "You might want to take a job with a big-time law firm for a few years, learn the ropes, build a résumé, and then get back into it." I agreed that sounded like a good plan.

It was a boom time for private law firms, and they needed Harvard grads—even oddballs like me. I joined one of the biggest old-line firms in Boston, Gaston Snow and Ely Bartlett, as a litigation associate. Little did I understand then that the practice of law was transforming from a profession for generalists to a business for specialists. Litigation meant wading through piles and boxes and cabinets of documents. Creativity was reserved for twisting precedents and looking for loopholes. My 9-to-5 law school drudgery became an 8-to-8 sweatshop, six days a week. So much for my rich and satisfying after-hours life of volunteer work.

I was unhappy at Gaston Snow, but not enough to be looking for a new job. I was suffering sufficiently—I figured I had to be on the right track. Just stick it out for a few more years. But then love intervened. My wife-to-be, Debra, was graduating from Harvard Business School and was heading to Palo Alto, California, to work at Hewlett-Packard. Gaston had an office just down the street in Silicon Valley. I maneuvered for a job there, got it, and off we went.

Adventures in the Valley

It was 1983. All that I knew about Silicon Valley came from a *Time* cover story about Apple Computer. But as soon as I arrived, I realized I had landed in a place where important things were happening. Silicon Valley was a haven for independent thinkers. Better yet, it was a place where people liked to come up with, and bet on, big ideas. If you bet right, you could win big—no matter your age, title, or years of experience.

My new environment felt exactly right, but I still had that messy career question to work out. Sure, a bright young person could get ahead in Silicon Valley—but what about a bright young lawyer? I wasn't optimistic. More important, I wasn't even sure that I wanted to continue being a lawyer at all, stuck in an office, doing the dreary paperwork of a legal specialist while, outside, intellectual fireworks were exploding.

Right from the beginning, my clients at the Palo Alto office of Gaston Snow were mostly young software programmers. They weren't astute businesspeople by and large, but they had talent, and they were inventing the future in their garages. From my days managing rock musicians, I had a good sense of how to relate to programmers. I knew what made them tick—their love of creative work and their uneasiness with commerce—and how I could help them build success from their ideas. We were a good match.

But Gaston Snow was struggling. Within a couple of years, I jumped ship to another firm, San Francisco-based Farella Braun & Martel. The partners there valued their personal and intellectual freedom; they often changed specialties when they became bored, even at the expense of the bottom line. Perhaps I had found a high-powered, prestigious law firm where I fit in, I told myself.

I had the good fortune in my first year to land a big client and a big deal. George Lucas was selling Pixar, then a high-end graphics hardware business, to Steve

Jobs, who had recently left Apple. By that time, I had transformed myself from a litigator into a "technology lawyer," which is another way of saying I was a jack-of-all-trades who could define, protect, and trade in intellectual property. I had worked my way into a hot specialty.

In the midst of the Pixar deal, I warmed to the idea that I had finally found a kind of law I could practice. But looking back now, I realized I was just basking in the glow of the deal's celebrities. In the end, it was too distant.

I remember the night the Pixar deal closed. There was a party in the firm's fanciest conference room. Champagne flowed, people laughed and congratulated one another. But while the clients joked and cavorted, I was elsewhere—in the document room down the hall, to be exact—making sure the deal's i's were dotted and the t's crossed. As I looked at the party through glass walls, I stewed. I wanted to be in their room writing the script, not in another room filing it.

If I had had an inkling about my true self, I might have moved on right then. Instead, I just persisted in a state of confusion. I told myself I had found an area of law in which I was skilled. I liked my coworkers. I was making more money than I needed. But I couldn't deny that I was unhappy. I was marching along to someone else's drummer.

Again, my plan was to stick it out, but it just so happened that counsel for one of the other parties in the Pixar deal noticed my work and recommended me to Apple, which was looking for in-house counsel. Even though I had no intention of taking the job—if anything, I wanted Apple as a client for my firm—I went on the interview. After all, I was a Harvard lawyer, and I had been taught well that the high art of law took place in private firms. In-house practice was for attorneys who couldn't hack it. The problem was, the people at Apple were infectious with creativity. They believed they were changing the world, not just selling computers and surely not just researching case law. Unexpectedly, my resistance to working in-house started to melt away. How bad could it be?

Very, according to my colleagues at Farella. When I told them about my offer from Apple, they were aghast. How could I jettison such a promising career? I would never be able to get back on the high road, they warned. I was settling for mediocrity. If I just stuck with private practice, they argued, all the bounty of being a prestigious partner would eventually be mine.

The next day, completely at a loss, I rode my bicycle mile after mile through the golden hills of Marin County. I have always been an avid rider and do some of my best thinking in the saddle. But 75 miles later, I had no better idea of what to do.

The answer came to me first thing the next morning. I walked into the office and, in a glance, saw my future. There, lining Farella's hallway, were the offices of the associates, then the junior partners, followed by the senior partners, crowned at the end by the managing partner. Nothing about the tidy scene excited me. In fact, it made me groan. I yearned for the energy that Apple was offering me. I quit that week.

In Apple's Core

In 1986, Apple was on a tear. The Macintosh was going strong, and the company was ripe with opportunities. Officially, I was a lawyer working in the firm's small but efficient legal department. But with encouragement from my boss—and Apple's senior managers—I dove into deal making.

With every deal, with every day, I learned more. I learned about the high-tech industry. I learned how large organizations think, make decisions, and operate. I had never been exposed to a corporation's internal machinations before, and I was senior enough in the company—eventually becoming senior counsel for half the business—that I was exposed to it all.

But the fun was over almost as quickly as it had started. A year after I joined, Apple decided to reorganize its internal legal function to reduce costs. I could stay, but I'd be back to practicing law. No way. I had been bitten by the business bug. For the first time in my career, I decided I would actually go in search of new work. I'd change directions. That was okay.

But before I could start sending out résumés, I got a tip: within days, Apple would announce the spin-off of its software applications group. It would be run by Bill Campbell, then Apple's executive vice president of sales and marketing. (Campbell is now chairman of Intuit.) Its mission would be to free Apple from its dependence on Microsoft software.

I knew Bill only by reputation. He was called "The Coach," ostensibly because he had been a coach of the Columbia University football team, but really because he was known to be an ardent mentor to his direct reports. He had a no-nonsense style—tough and tireless but warmhearted, too. I decided working for him might not be a bad idea.

When I finally got to meet with Bill, he was on the run, as usual. He pulled me into a dark conference room, and, without turning on the lights, gave me the three-minute pitch. He was going to build a world-class software company focused on the Macintosh and using the products that Apple was making. The new company would have its own culture, compensation, and infrastructure, and within three years he expected to take the company public. Was I in?

Three minutes in the dark, and this guy wanted me to make a life-changing career decision. He hadn't discussed my title, salary, or even my role. With only a moment's hesitation, the word came out of my mouth. "Yes."

"Great. You're the first co-founder," said Bill, his voice trailing off as he took off down the hall. "Let's get moving."

Intellectually, I knew what I had done was insane. But I was enamored with the idea of joining a start-up. And, I asked myself, if nothing careful or planned had ever worked in my career before, why start now? I would just have to get used to feeling uneasy.

But what a great move I had made—in fact, it was one of the best of my life. First, I learned more about business in the three years that followed than most people learn in 20. Second, I found a lifelong friend and mentor in Bill. Third, and as important, I learned the virtue of following your passion, of obeying your gut. Bit by little bit, I was letting go of the notion of a linear, logical career path.

Intellectually, I knew what I had done was insane. But I was enamored with the idea of joining a start-up.

The new company was called Claris Corporation, and it opened up for me a universe of experiences. I kept my legal role as some basis for credibility on the management team, but I grabbed every other function or job that wasn't taken or promised. I secured a facility, set up the compensation and benefits plans, and negotiated the separation agreement with Apple. I bought companies, like FileMaker, that became mainstays of the business. I bought products, like ClarisWorks and AppleWorks GS, that made us a full-fledged software player. I helped strategize and structure our international operations and offices. And as secretary to the board, I learned how that critical body works.

Best of all, I got to work closely with Bill, and that taught me the importance of attaching yourself to great people, great teachers. Before, I had focused on jobs and opportunities. Now, watching Bill in action every day, I realized that it mattered just as much—more, even—to find a talented, experienced mentor who is willing to invest the time and effort to develop you as a person and a businessman. Not that working with Bill was always easy. In fact, we often clashed at the beginning. After all, I was still a lawyer at heart. I wanted things to be buttoned down, methodical, and tightly structured. But Bill always put people first. When I wanted to talk about deals, he counseled me to think about relationships. When I wanted to focus on the bottom line, Bill urged me to think about individuals. He should have fired me a hundred times. Instead, he invested countless hours into making me realize—slowly but surely—the error of my ways.

Bill showed me the power of leadership. I often wonder, if I had followed the career path ahead of me at Farella Braun & Martel, or even as an in-house lawyer at Apple, would I have ever seen that light? Maybe—but perhaps not for a dozen more years. There are just not that many exceptional leaders around—particularly not in the legal field, where most firms are loose confederacies of individual contributors. But when I took that leap of faith to follow Bill, I dove, too, into one of life's most important lessons. People will deliver the impossible if you inspire them. And inspiration is a subtle art—a mix of empathy, respect, and love. You can only learn it from a master.

Bill was and still is a master. Under his leadership, Claris grew in three years to a profitable global company, with nearly $90 million in revenues and more than 700 employees. We decided to go public in 1990. Goldman Sachs worked with us to prepare the offering. But in the process, Apple realized that to be successful as an independent company, Claris would have to sell Windows products as well. Apple panicked and exercised its option to buy back Claris at a premium. At first, members of the top team were overjoyed with the news; we were all going to be wealthy. But in a matter of days, those feelings were mixed with sadness. We realized that we would never work together again—the magic was over, and it was priceless.

I would now rise through the corporate ranks in one of the technology era's most dynamic companies, right? Wrong.

In the aftermath of the sale, Apple offered me a sizable raise and promotion to stay on at Claris in a business role. That was good news, I reasoned. It proved I had established a career path in the high-tech industry. I could now rise through the corporate ranks in one of the most visible and dynamic companies of the new technology era. A career at last.

Wrong. I just could not stay on a career path to save my life. As I weighed the Apple offer, I got a call from Bill Campbell, who had become CEO of GO Corporation. At the time, GO was full of hype, talent, and money. It was going to revolutionize the PC business by introducing the first pen-based computer. Did I want to come along for the ride? Bill asked.

This time I paused long enough to ask what my position would be. Bill thought for a second, then said CFO. I was shocked. I had a rudimentary understanding of FASB and GAAP, but I had no accounting or systems experience. When I asked Bill to explain himself, he told me he was looking for a partner—someone to make deals and help manage internal operations while he drove the company externally. I would be able to hire all the expertise I needed. What he wanted was my broad experience, my deal-making ability, and my friendship. "You've got it," I told him.

This time, my gut steered me into a tidal wave of stress. Within days at GO, I realized we had six weeks of cash left. Six weeks! And this was in the high-tech venture-capital depression of 1991, not the euphoric Internet capital markets of 1999. We scrambled. First, we decided to exit the hardware business and mimic Microsoft. I spent a harried weekend learning to run a spreadsheet, grabbing every Microsoft 10K and 10Q form I could get my hands on, and modeling GO's software business all the way down to the product level. We also decided to sell GO's hardware business to a new venture with AT&T—for exactly $10 million. We closed in the nick of time, and I hoped that my fund-raising days were over.

They weren't. GO's product was delayed, and we needed a truckload more money just a few months later. Eventually, we raised $75 million, but we never managed to ship a commercially viable product. From the start of the second year, I couldn't see how we could continue to raise these huge sums of money. We had to sell, which we did in 1993.

At GO, despite all its difficulties, Bill had groomed me to be a CEO by giving me a diverse set of management responsibilities. But the fact was, I no longer had the compelling drive to be a big gun. At age 39, I was struck by how little time was left for the rest of my life. I was always sprinting, always on deadline, always in the critical path, subsisting on adrenaline and caffeine. I had no time for reading, cooking, traveling, music, and art, and little time for my steadfast wife and lovable hounds. If you looked in the bank, I was well off. But I still felt poor, incomplete.

My musings about life and work—and balance—came to an abrupt halt with a call from a headhunter.

From my vantage point today, I see that my exit from GO was the beginning of my slow realization that life cannot be compartmentalized. I was working like a madman but spending very little time on things that mattered to me. In society, we call obsessive-compulsive behavior a disorder. People take medication to combat it. But when we demonstrate obsessive-compulsive behavior about work and making money, it is considered completely normal, a "sacred hunger," and is amply rewarded. I was a case in point, and somewhere deep inside me, I was starting to ask, "What is wrong with this picture?"

No happy ending—not yet. My musings about life and work—and balance—came to an abrupt halt with a call from a headhunter. He wanted to know if I would be interested in meeting with LucasArts Entertainment, the digital products division of George Lucas's empire. LucasArts made games and "edutainment" products. Finally, I thought, here's my chance to take that next step up the ladder and be the CEO that I had been groomed to be. My life could wait.

I donned an ill-fitting, out-of-fashion suit from my lawyer days and interviewed with the hiring committee. On paper, I did not meet their specifications at all: not a game aficionado, no real P&L experience, no background in the entertainment business. Still, they invited me to meet with George Lucas at his SkyWalker Ranch a few days later. We had a highly spirited exchange about the future of the gaming and entertainment industries, two topics I found fascinating despite my relative naiveté. I left the session not knowing Lucas's predilections toward me, but a few days later, the job was mine to refuse. I grabbed it.

LucasArts presented a very different challenge than Claris or GO. For one thing, I had no mentor. George controlled the company, and the board was much more of a kitchen cabinet than an independent-minded group of advisers. Entertainment was also a new industry for me, and the aggressive, equity-based approach to building businesses that I learned in Silicon Valley was at odds with the cautious, cash-flow mentality of the film business. The LucasArts culture was insular, and I had an uphill battle establishing myself in it.

Still, I loved the people at LucasArts, the highly creative writers, animators, musicians, artists, and programmers. There was a buzz about the place that kept me electrified. We made bold moves, restructuring our distribution system and installing our own sales force. We experimented with CD-ROMs and entered into a strategic partnership with Nintendo. It was a lot of change for the conservative businesspeople at LucasArts, but it worked. In less than two years, sales more than tripled and profits soared even faster. I was liking this CEO thing.

But there was a dark side. George was focused on the *Star Wars* movies that were in the works. The company was doing so well that, despite his initial promises, it looked unlikely that LucasArts would go public or be spun off; in other words, I would never have the autonomy I craved. And much to my chagrin, the board blocked any acquisitions that I suggested.

When a headhunter from Crystal Dynamics called about the CEO job at the three-year-old video game company in Silicon Valley, I was ready to listen. I would have lots of independence, I was promised, plus a higher salary than at LucasArts, and more stock, too. As an added bonus, Crystal was a mere 15 minutes from my home rather than the 75-minute commute each way to LucasArts. This would be my most logical career move yet—CEO to CEO, game business to game business, back in the Valley, and a raise to boot.

It turned out to be the worst career move I ever made. Production schedules that had been set before I arrived were ridiculously tight; we couldn't hit them. Crystal's board was unwieldy—a nine-person collection of founders, venture capitalists, ex-Crystal CEOs, and industry partners. But the biggest problem was that I had no passion for the business. I wanted to transform Crystal into a creative leader in cinematic digital entertainment, more like LucasArts. Given the exigencies of the marketplace, however, the smart move was to shrink it into a niche video-game maker. One year after I arrived, I resigned.

Time Out

It was 1996. I was 42. And I was in free fall. After all, I hadn't left Crystal with a gold star on my forehead. I'd bailed out after posting a less than admirable performance. Who would want me? What next?

One option was to commit myself full time to serving on boards. I was already sitting on a handful, and I could easily ramp up. But that idea didn't excite me. I didn't want to go out to pasture, not yet. My career wasn't over—I wasn't even sure it had begun. The other option was to say yes to any one of the headhunters calling me about CEO positions in the Internet ventures that were springing up like California poppies in April. Again, the answer was no.

Finally, after incessant years of go, go, go, I wanted to pause. I wanted to figure out what I wanted to be. Without actually realizing it, I had given up on the idea of a career. What was a career anyway? I had had a lot of fascinating jobs; I had built a life to be proud of. It was time to let go of the notion of climbing and just accept the fact that I was on a long and winding journey. Where I went next was entirely my choice.

So I was free to decide my next step. Did that make me feel great? No—I was scared witless. For the first time in ages, I had no identity. No company to attach to my name at parties. No title to bring with me when I left the house. I dreaded meeting new people and having to explain myself without a flimsy two-by-three inch card stating that I was "President" or "CEO."

Months of thinking went by. My terror ebbed and flowed, mostly flowed. I wondered if I was going to fritter away the rest of my life considering my alternatives. I wondered if I should go back to the manual labor that had made me so happy during my part-time jobs in high school and college. Maybe I could be a chef, I thought. At least then I'd have medical benefits again. I'd have a job title.

Then, one day, I got a call from my old friend Steve Perlman. The CEO of WebTV at the time, Steve was a highly charismatic visionary who had never run a company before. I was already on WebTV's board, but Steve asked me if I'd do more—if I would support him day-to-day as he built his company. The role we agreed on was supposed to be part-time and temporary. I'd be an adviser, a mentor, or something like that. We'd figure it out as we went.

As it ended up, I loved the work. I got to spend all my time doing the 20% of the CEO role that was truly exciting to me—strategizing, building relationships, making deals, and mentoring teams. And I didn't have to get near the 80% of the role that I found so tedious and draining—the tactical stuff. Six months in, I decided I loved the work so much that I should do more of it. I could be a virtual CEO for a portfolio of companies—if I could find takers.

I did. Since I put out my shingle as a virtual CEO, I have had the opportunity to look at hundreds of new businesses. I choose my jobs based on one thing—call it the thump factor. If an entrepreneur and his plan make my heart pound, I sign on. So far, I've worked with an Internet chat community, a digital animation studio, an on-line party-supply store, a personalized television company, a Web promotions service, a small-business applications service provider, a nationwide on-line infomediary for child and elder care services, a broadband and broadcast TV news syndicator, a Web-based customer-satisfaction business, an Internet invitations service, and a streaming-audio audience measurement and targeting company. Some of the ventures have taken off, others have floundered, but all of them have captured my heart and imagination. In return, I've poured myself into each of them.

What, then, of that life I wanted—with cooking, reading, and the like? I do a lot more of those things now. In fact, I try to travel for pleasure a couple of months a year. I call my life "integrated." I don't have a job, I have work that weaves in and out of my life as I guide it.

In arriving at my noncareer career, two major issues have become clear for me. First, I have had to learn to live with a murky business identity. Few people get what I mean when I say "virtual CEO," but that's part of the price I pay for my choices. There is no "handle" that excuses people from actually getting to know me—Randy Komisar, the person, not the title—if they want to work with me. Second, I have come to see that living modestly must be a deliberate choice in this time and place—it's like a discipline. Here in Silicon Valley, we live among centamillionaires and billionaires. There is intense pressure to keep up—to live very large. But part of letting go of career chasing is also letting go of status. That, too, can be a shock to the system at first, but it quickly begins to feel fantastic—utterly liberating. Today, my comfortable lifestyle is dictated by what I

Don't let a career drive you, let passion drive your life. That may not get you up any ladder, but it will make your trip down a long and winding road more interesting.

need to be happy, not what society prescribes as the trappings of success. I don't have a big, fancy house. I drive a used motorcycle; it was a great deal. When I eat out, which I do a lot, I favor ethnic restaurants over Chez Panisse. I travel economy, not first class. None of these feel like sacrifices. They feel like rewards for the life that I've remade. They reflect who I am, not what others say I should be. Once you have an inkling about what truly makes you happy, it becomes a lot easier to reprioritize and spend your most precious asset—time—on the qualitative experiences that fulfill you. And that's more satis-fying than squandering time on meaningless work just so you can acquire the redundant artifacts of material success.

WHEN ALL IS SAID AND DONE, perhaps I am not really in a great position to give career advice given the fact that I haven't had one. But for what it's worth, here's a final bit anyway: If you can do anything setting out, or along the way—because it's never too late to start again—figure out who you are. What do you love to do? How do you want to live? Then, don't let a career drive you, let passion drive your life. That may not get you up any ladder, but it will make your trip down a long and winding road more interesting. And in the end, if it makes you feel better, go ahead and call it a career. It doesn't matter. A career is what you make it.

Originally published in March 2000
Reprint R00207

The Right Way to Be Fired

LAURENCE J. STYBEL AND
MARYANNE PEABODY

Executive Summary

NEARLY ALL OF US WILL LOSE our jobs sometime, but is there a right way to be terminated? What differentiates fired employees who make the best of their situations from those who do not? One answer is mind-set. Many workers unconsciously hold a "tenure mind-set," believing in the promise of employment security. By contrast, other workers hold an "assignment mentality," seeking each job as one in a series of impermanent, career building stepping-stones. Most corporate board members and CEOs have this latter mind-set and consider their executives to be filling terminal assignments; people who possess this mentality usually rebound swiftly when fired.

But when employees who hold a tenure mind-set are suddenly fired or laid off, the authors say, they can fall into three common traps. Executives who have overidentified with their jobs and feel indispensable to their

49

organizations get caught in the "lost identity" trap; they react to termination with anger and bitterness. In the "lost family" trap, employees possess tight-knit, emotional bonds with coworkers. When terminated, they feel betrayed and rejected. And finally, some introverted executives fall into the "lost ego" trap; they quietly retreat without negotiating fair termination packages and may settle for less satisfying work the next time around.

To prepare for the eventuality of termination, the authors suggest that executives adopt the assignment mind-set at all times. They should keep their social networks alive, include a termination clause in employment contracts, and consider hiring an agent. If warning signs warrant, they might even volunteer to be terminated. By assuming control over the way they are fired, people can gain control over their careers.

EVEN IN THE BEST OF TIMES, executives get fired, and in the worst, they get fired with disquieting frequency. Indeed, as the economy softens, you only have to glance at the newspaper to see layoffs left, right, and center, mainly to cut costs. You can be a top performer today and still lose your job. The question is: Can you lose it the right way?

For 22 years, we have worked closely with more than 500 senior executives in dozens of industries to manage their careers in good times and in bad. Over and over, we have observed how executives react to being fired or laid off. The majority handle termination with dignity, even elegance. They negotiate handsome severance packages, part with their employers on amicable terms, and position themselves for their next assignments. Yet some executives take actions that subsequently backfire, setting the stage for difficulty in procuring new jobs—and even destroying their careers.

What differentiates fired employees who make the best of their situations from those who do not? One answer is mind-set. Virtually every executive feels shock and anger upon losing a job, but those who rebound swiftly have usually absorbed what we call an "assignment mentality"; they see each job as a stepping-stone, a temporary career-building project. That's good, because most corporate boards and CEOs have this

Fired executives who rebound swiftly have usually absorbed an assignment mentality: They see each job as a stepping-stone, a temporary career-building project.

mind-set, too, a continuing phenomenon that emerged about 20 years ago. Most leaders see an executive in the ranks—even the best performers—as filling an assignment. When it's over—for strategic or financial reasons—so is the executive's tenure with the company.

On an intellectual level, most executives know that the assignment mentality rules. Even so, some allow that reality to recede in their minds; it's only human nature. Then they get fired or are laid off and, like clockwork, fall into one of three traps. The first is the "lost identity" trap. Executives in this group have, over months or years, allowed themselves to "become" their jobs. Unable to imagine their companies existing without them or themselves existing without their companies, they react to termination with rage, even vengeance. The second is the "lost family" trap, the province of executives who believe that their coworkers are more than that—dear friends, even a second family. Under these circumstances,

termination becomes painful estrangement, with atten-
dant feelings of betrayal and sorrow. Finally, there is the
"lost ego" trap, in which executives silently retreat from
the company without negotiating fair termination packages and disappear into troughs of silent despair that
make them reluctant to reach for the next opportunities.

We'll examine these traps, all of which can arise from
being fired or laid off, in the following pages and then
turn to a few strategies for making a dignified departure.
But first, a few observations about the assignment mentality itself.

Which Mind-Set Do You Have?

The assignment model common in most companies
today got its start in project-oriented industries—such
as the arts, sports, agriculture, construction, and consulting. In these arenas, work comes and goes; individuals
are contracted as needed; and work groups are continually assembled, altered, and dissolved. The assignment
model presupposes the existence of "assignment executives"—people hired for two to six years to guide and
implement a company's strategy. Sometimes, a company
itself may be on assignment, in the sense that its end is
foreseeable: For example, a company faced with a short
product life cycle, tough competition, or an unforgiving
investment community may develop a corporate exit
strategy. Such an exit strategy might be to increase
shareholder value by 50% and then engineer an initial
public offering or an acquisition by a larger competitor.
Once this strategy is successful, a new group of senior
managers replaces the outgoing one.

Although the assignment model is real, it is rarely discussed. A mythic belief lives alongside it in the minds of

most employees. This is the "tenure mind-set"—the comforting sense that an organization willingly parts with valued employees only when they formally retire. It has long been dead in corporate America, although most companies won't openly admit it. After all, letting employees know that their jobs are finite would make them feel disposable and would hurt recruiting efforts. For this reason, most companies perpetuate the tenure myth, particularly in corporate literature. Annual reports and other accounts, filled with glowing language about career paths, continually work to persuade employees that companies take long-term views of their career development.

Most of the time, the assignment and tenure mind-sets coexist peacefully. Externally hired CEOs truly understand that their jobs are pure assignments, because very specific termination and severance clauses are written into the employment contracts. For everyone else, the assignment nature of the job may not be clearly understood. Indeed, it's easy to ignore, even to deny. Moreover, senior executives tend to believe their own jobs are the most secure. And it isn't unusual for a founder, a CEO, or an executive promoted from within to be lulled into the tenure mind-set. When the company's exit strategy dictates a departure and sets in motion a collision between the two mind-sets, disillusionment can emerge and executives can fall into one of the three traps.

Caught in the Quagmire

When terminated suddenly, even the most widely admired and competent executives can be overcome by anger and grief. Saddled by these emotional responses, they may take actions they later regret. Let's take a closer look at these three traps.

THE LOST IDENTITY TRAP

The people most susceptible to this trap are likely to have been with a company for some time; their jobs may have been cut short due to a sudden change in course or a pressing financial crisis. Such people often include founders and senior executives who have achieved positions of power through promotion. In the day-to-day demands of doing their jobs, executives who fall into this trap have nurtured the strong sense that they are indispensable; they may have heard as much from investors or board members. Confronted with sudden job loss, they fall apart and often lash out against the former company—now rife with "enemies."

Consider Fred, a 31-year-old engineer who received his degree from MIT and then spent three years working for a large computer manufacturer. There, he developed a key technology that allowed companies to tap into their large databases via the Internet. After inventing the software, Fred decided to found a company with his own sweat equity; in time, he accepted funding from a venture capital firm with the understanding that he would be surrendering control of day-to-day operations to one of the venture partners. The partner said that Fred's continued presence was extremely important and that he hoped that Fred would consider assuming the role of chairman. Eager to finance his company, Fred agreed.

Eventually, the VC firm hired a permanent CEO, a 54-year-old man who had plenty of managerial experience but who lacked the technical skills that Fred so prized in himself. When he wanted to drive home a point, the CEO called Fred "son"; in response, Fred would mutter, "I already have a father." One day, the CEO and the VC met with Fred and fired him.

A few weeks later, Fred told us angrily, "I was kicked out of my own company." By then, Fred had done a lot of damage. In the days after his termination, he phoned each of the partners of the VC firm and accused them of betrayal. He refused to pass on his operational or engineering knowledge to anyone within the company. And when an industry analyst called to find out what had happened, Fred "secretly" confided his anger and frustration. Soon, word of Fred's unprofessional behavior circulated in both the large software industry and the small VC community. Eventually, Fred created a new start-up software company but, stamped as a person no one wanted to make deals with, was unable to secure further VC funding.

THE LOST FAMILY TRAP

This trap is most prevalent among people working in fields like marketing or magazine publishing or within start-ups—all environments of high emotional intensity. Employees in such organizations can form tight-knit, emotional bonds, just as troops in combat do. These bonds can become so close that relationships with people outside work may seem dull.

Like the main character in the 1970s sitcom *The Mary Tyler Moore Show*, executives with such intense connections can make work the emotional center of their universe. Projecting familial roles upon colleagues, who become surrogate parents, siblings, aunts, or uncles, these executives suffer grief when, on termination, the "old gang" suddenly grows distant. But who can blame the coworkers? Suffering from survivor guilt and perhaps worrying about losing their own jobs, they're instinctively turning away from the person in pain. The coworkers, too, are in shock. Executives, however, caught emotionally in the lost family trap, can't see this. They feel as if friendships have been severed and they've been rejected. As a result, they sink into bitterness and depression.

Justine was the CEO of a consumer goods manufacturing company that had once dominated its marketplace. A 15-year veteran of her company, she was an energetic workaholic who felt alive only when she was at work. Justine loved her husband and children, but she found family life mundane compared with the adrenaline-pumping game of business. Over time, however, the company began losing market share. Although the members of the board liked Justine, they felt that the company needed to go in a completely new direction by taking its manufacturing offshore; Justine fought this idea because it meant shutting down facilities and laying off beloved workers. The board, impatient to reposition the company to take advantage of new opportunities, unanimously voted to let Justine go and replace her with a new CEO.

On an intellectual level, Justine understood that anyone can be fired. As head of the company, she had arranged enough terminations to know how the game is played. But upon being fired herself, Justine believed she had lost not only her job and income but also the de facto family of which she believed herself the matriarch. When she reached out to her former subordinates, whom she had protected and befriended, they did not have time to meet her for drinks or dinner and seemed uninterested in how she was faring. The truth was that her "family" was afraid to go near her for fear that merely associating with Justine would bring them to the board's attention.

Unable to hide her depression and bitterness, Justine became an unattractive candidate. Recruiters felt she had failed to manage her board properly and hadn't rebounded from an event that should have been predictable. Unable to find work, Justine purchased a franchise retail operation, whose employees became a replacement family—and from which she could never be fired.

THE LOST EGO TRAP

Executives who fall into the lost ego trap, in our observations, tend to be introverts. Such people work very effectively in areas of the company such as accounting and finance, R&D, manufacturing, or engineering, which don't demand high levels of socialization with outside constituencies. After being unexpectedly terminated, these executives tend to withdraw.

Consider Frank, a CFO for a retail company with $50 million in sales. As a child, Frank was shy and had few friends; although he loved playing the piano, he never enjoyed public performance. After majoring in math in college, Frank earned his CPA and followed a career in finance, eventually attaining the rank of CFO. He became the acting head of the company when the CEO, after a bitter divorce, escaped on his sailboat to cruise around the world and enjoy an extended vacation on a tropical island. Although Frank was competent enough to earn the owner's trust during this long sabbatical, he was not able to prevent a loss of market share when the economy hit tough times. The fall in the company's fortunes forced the CEO to cut short his holiday; upon his return, he fired Frank and resumed control of the business with an eye toward selling it.

Although he had been with the company for 12 years, Frank reacted to the news of his termination and scant severance without a complaint and quietly left, not wanting to make a fuss. It never occurred to him to consult an attorney skilled in severance negotiations for help in procuring a more generous termination package. Every book he read on job hunting recommended networking, but he just couldn't do it; he felt that the books were telling him to be someone he wasn't. Instead of reaching out to acquaintances or taking advantage of professional networks, he relied on third parties such as recruiters or on electronic job boards to find his next position; but these efforts produced few results.

Finally, an opportunity developed with a company 150 miles away from his home. Frank listened lackadaisically as the recruiter described the position. He was already conjuring the negative aspects of the deal. "I'll have to pull the kids out of school and away from all their friends," he thought. "My wife will have to quit the job she loves. We'll have to sell our wonderful home in an uncertain housing market." Frank told the recruiter he would think about it and hung up. But rather than balancing the imagined negatives with the job's prospective benefits—the stable and growing company, a generous relocation package, the excellent position with an equity stake—Frank focused only on the

By remaining conscious of the impermanence of their jobs, executives can avoid merely reacting and can adopt systematic approaches to the next move.

downsides, which combined into an excuse to turn down the prospect without further consideration. Eventually, he accepted a far less promising position within ten miles of his house.

Exiting with Aplomb

Executives can fall into these traps—of fighting back, mourning, or fading away—when they are reacting to sudden or unexpected events. Better, of course, to be prepared, and in a moment, we'll talk about how to do that. But first, here's a piece of tactical advice. When fired or being laid off, follow the old saying and count to 100 to cool down. That is, resist the impulse to say the first thing that comes into your mind. In fact, try not to say much of anything. Contact an attorney who negotiates severance packages for senior executives. Do not call colleagues, send e-mails, or speak to reporters. In the next 48 hours, people will be contacting you. Say nothing until the severance contract has been signed. It is also important that your spouse or partner stick to whatever "official story" is being developed about you and the company.

That's the short-term fix. Now let's explore long-term strategies for departing correctly. These strategies all involve a proactive—even calculated—approach to termination. They also require adoption of the assignment mind-set: by remaining conscious of the impermanence of their jobs, executives will avoid merely reacting and can adopt systematic approaches to the next move.

Rhonda exemplifies an executive who handled her termination the right way. As a child, she had been raised to believe the adage, "If you take care of the company, the company will take care of you." After completing her MBA, she moved to San Francisco and worked at a midsized software company. When she and all her colleagues lost their jobs during an acquisition, Rhonda reevaluated her tenure mind-set. The experience persuaded her that the familiar adage was no longer tenable, and she learned to treat successive opportunities as moves toward her career goal of becoming a successful CEO.

Eventually, a new e-commerce venture with a focus on distribution hired Rhonda as its CEO. A top-tier VC firm had proffered the first financing round of $3 million and also promised a second round of $7 million. Rhonda—now armed with assignment thinking—negotiated a one-year severance package at full pay as part of the employment contract. Soon afterward, she began growing the company, and the VC partner expressed satisfaction with her efforts. But instead of nursing illusions of permanence, Rhonda kept a weather eye out for signs of the company's approaching exit strategy. She likened her assignment to "parachuting onto a sailboat during a typhoon—I just landed with my hands on the tiller and went from there." Aware of the perilousness of e-commerce ventures, she cultivated her network for the day when she would need it. She served on two corporate boards, one a computer hardware company and the other a wireless communications company, and spent one night every two weeks staying in touch by phone with top business contacts. These were upbeat conversations; she never complained to other executives about her work.

In the spring of 2000, when the Internet bubble burst, the VC partner announced that not only would his firm not put in the $7 million but that it also wanted the whole operation shut down as soon as possible. Of course, Rhonda was angry at the partner for reneging on his promise. But she kept her negative feelings to herself; they passed soon enough, for she was well positioned for the next assignment. The venture capitalist was so impressed by Rhonda's behavior that he wrote a glowing letter of recommendation that complemented her own efforts to procure a new assignment as CEO of a new distribution company with ample financing and a strong market position.

The single most important key to Rhonda's success was her assignment mentality. Although the tenure mind-set had felt natural and comforting to her, she understood that even the most desirable job today is finite. She also understood that she was responsible for crafting her own exit strategy.

In managing current assignments and protecting options for the future, executives can follow Rhonda's example by adopting the following strategies. While not surprising or new, these tasks can be forgotten or postponed by executives too enmeshed in day-to-day work to take care of their careers. And these tactics can prove invaluable during termination.

The insertion of a termination clause at the time of hire feels completely counterintuitive. Nevertheless, it's your best hedge against a bitter exit.

INSERT A TERMINATION CLAUSE IN YOUR EMPLOYMENT CONTRACT

A new hire is never more attractive to the company than on the day before signing an employment contract; that's when you best control the terms of your employment. If you are newly hired or in the process of being promoted to a position that requires signing a new employment or confidentiality contract, it's possible to build your exit terms into the agreement. Like a prenuptial agreement that protects both sides if a marriage is dissolved, the insertion of such a clause at the time of hire feels completely counterintuitive. Nevertheless, it's your best hedge against a bitter exit. Hire a lawyer with experience in employment contract negotiation to insert clauses that will provide a satisfactory exit package in the event of termination.

SCHEDULE NETWORK CALLS

Make networking a discipline, not a catch-as-catch-can activity. In an assignment-driven world, keeping one's network of professional acquaintances intact is time-consuming, but it's a critical cost of doing business. The importance of networking is obvious—which may be why managers, who sometimes put their own career needs on hold, rarely think of it. Unless network calls are explicitly scheduled and rigorously carried out, they can remain mere intentions. A biweekly calendar note reminds you to get in touch with the important people in your network—especially those with their own strong networks such as valued advisers to CEOs or partners within law, consulting, or accounting firms.

RAISE YOUR VISIBILITY—BY STEALTH

Most executives understand that if they conduct personal self-branding PR campaigns, their companies will automatically fire them; the only person with official sanction to "represent" the company is likely to be the CEO. On occasion, your company's public relations team may be able to provide you with speaking engagements or bylined articles in trade publications; but such opportunities can be rare.

That's where stealth comes in. You may not be able to talk to reporters, but you can certainly raise your visibility with other professionals. You can serve on for-profit boards, at least one of which should be in an industry other than your own. This is so important that we routinely suggest adding a clause requiring board service into an employment contract. In addition to garnering useful perspectives from peers in other arenas, serving on industry boards expands the network both within and beyond one's core business—making it possible to move into new companies and industries later on. You can also play a selective and strategic leadership role in a trade association. By volunteering for externally oriented committees—such as membership, marketing, legislative affairs, or programs—you'll be able to get in front of outside constituencies while retaining a strong industry profile.

WATCH FOR EXIT SIGNS

Being terminated should not come as a surprise, but it sometimes does. Some companies provide no warning to employees about to be terminated, for fear that advance notice may result in damage to the company—from sabotage of computer systems, for example. To be as prepared as possible, pay attention to your company's culture of termination (see "Auf Wiedersehen: How to Fire Right" at the end of this article). Are people severed harshly and hustled out of the building, or is the door left open for a possible return? If the former, you may want to raise your guard and take some proactive steps.

Likewise, watch for how the company itself is planning to exit, because your job depends on it. Examine the position and assignment changes within the company; do position descriptions or sets of responsibilities—including your own—imply an end? If yours does, it's entirely fair to ask whether your position will continue or how it will change once this particular work is complete. It's also helpful to cultivate a strong relationship with a founder or another trusted adviser who has "seen it all before" and who can help you stay aware of prospective changes. Remember—if you think you are about to be fired, you probably are. But if you are confused by signals being given to you, consider hiring an executive coach to help you sort them out (see "Do You Need an Agent?" at the end of this article).

VOLUNTEER TO BE TERMINATED

If the company's exit strategy appears to include you, consider volunteering to be terminated before it occurs. By initiating such a discussion, you become the actor rather than the one who is acted upon. Here's what happened when Joe, the CEO of a large firm, volunteered to be laid off as his company was acquired. The terms of his existing contract allowed Joe to stay on for two years as president of the newly merged organization while the CEO of the acquiring company became chairman. But rather than waiting to be terminated after the contract expired, Joe approached the new chairman with a suggestion. Joe said that while he knew that the contract was a fair one, he fully appreciated that the acquiring company would want to run things differently. He offered to resign, provided that an excellent severance agreement could be developed. The chairman, delighted to be saved the trouble of firing Joe, was extraordinarily generous, and Joe's severance package allowed him to retire altogether.

WE DO NOT MEAN TO SUGGEST that executives become overly wary and move from job to job or from company to company too quickly; a lot of mobility is as damaging as a little. Rather, we posit that in most cases, a degree of self-interest in one's career—as understood in its broadest, life-spanning sense—is both healthy and necessary. Executives who hold on to the tenure myth may find it difficult to assume an assignment mentality, and understandably so. It's natural to want to believe that the company for which you work so hard cares about you. But allowing yourself to be lulled into a false sense of security sets you up for shock and disappointment when you are fired or laid off.

On the corporate level, terminations are among the most predictable crises in business. When you develop an assignment mind-set, your termination becomes predictable on a personal level, too. Then even an experience as negative as being fired can turn out to be strangely empowering. It's ironic, but true: When you assume control over the way you are fired, you can gain control over your career.

Auf Wiedersehen: How to Fire Right

EVERY INDUSTRY BOASTS companies with traditions of never rehiring people who leave, regardless of how well those employees perform. But given the growth of the

assignment mind-set within corporations, the unprecedented ease of movement between companies, and the
difficulty of attracting excellent employees, it no longer
makes sense to slam the door behind departed workers
who have been solid performers. After all, such employees do not simply vanish into the night. They go to professional meetings, where they can openly discuss their exit
treatment with prospective recruits. Customers, strategic
partners, distributors, or acquisition candidates may hire
them. And once the noncompete clauses in their employment contracts expire, they might even decide to work
for a competitor.

Many companies usher employees out the door with
minimal termination packages, even sending them off
under a cloud of humiliation. We call these "goodbye"
terminations, because they deal in finality. In one goodbye termination, a CEO who had had a disagreement
with the board was fired, although the company's press
release claimed he had resigned. The chairman then
issued an internal memo stating that the board had
forced the CEO to resign. Employees saw the ashen-
faced CEO clean out his desk and depart under the
gaze of the HR vice president. Not surprisingly, morale
within the company dropped precipitously, and several
valued employees also quit.

A much better alternative to the goodbye termination
is what we call the "auf Wiedersehen" (German for "until
we see you again") termination. An auf Wiedersehen
departure assumes that the company will meet the
departing employee again in another context and thus
conducts the termination as respectfully as possible.
There are several advantages to this approach. First, by
making an effort to preserve the employee's dignity and

goodwill, the company decreases the chance of a back-lash from the employee or of a sullied reputation for its act. Second, when there is a poor fit between an individual and a company, an auf Wiedersehen exit makes it easier for the employee to leave (or even quit) without causing trauma to the company or himself.

In addition, auf Wiedersehen terminations make it possible to re-recruit top-performing alumni. This makes excellent financial sense. According to the Corporate Leadership Council, it costs 176% of base salary to recruit and train a new IT professional and 241% of base salary to recruit and train a new middle manager. When alumni are re-recruited, costs drop to almost zero because companies don't have to pay search firms, inter-view candidates, train employees, or get them ramped up for productivity.

By keeping accurate performance records on past employees and staying in touch with excellent alumni, companies can also reduce the possibility of mis-hire, thus saving time and money. McKinsey, for example, sponsors alumni programs such as special breakfasts and on-line directories that allow former employees to keep in touch with the company and one another. Since alumni are also shareholders, the strong alumni-share-holder base has helped attract and retain shareholders during economic downturns.

Using an auf Wiedersehen termination policy doesn't necessarily mean that companies must spend huge amounts on termination benefits; it merely requires that companies treat departing employees with the same respect when they leave as they received when they entered. Your pay policies should also be consistent. In comparisons with your competition, don't brag that you pay at the 75th percentile for new hires but at the 50th percentile for terminations. Pay policies and termination policies are two sides of one coin called "how people are treated."

Do You Need An Agent?

CONSIDER THE FOLLOWING scenario: A recruiter calls you about a "fantastic" opportunity with another company, but you are too busy to give it serious attention. So you propose an alternative. "I want to give this opportunity the consideration it deserves," you say. "Given the demands of my current job, it would not be fair to my company to spend time with you. Let me give you the phone number of my agent. She understands what would be a good fit for me. My agent will do the initial screening. If the answer is yes, then we can talk in more detail. If it's no, I will be glad to refer you to others."

Tiger Woods benefits from having an agent, but a CEO? As far-fetched as it sounds, executive agents are part of a growing industry of coaches. The reason is simple. CEOs must focus their full attention on their current jobs, but in so doing, they forget to manage their careers. As a result, when assignments end, they can find themselves grasping at opportunities rather than making strategic moves.

A CEO agent helps clients with career strategy, presentation skills, image building, networking, and employment and salary negotiations. He or she also helps to screen job opportunities, even to manage money or save face in difficult situations. But is an executive agent necessary? As partners in an executive search, coaching, and outplacement firm, we can say, "Absolutely not." This kind of professional help makes little sense for extremely senior executives—CEOs like Jack Welch or Michael Dell, for example—who are very public symbols of their enterprises. Many groups within their corporations—such as the corporate public relations and investor relations departments, who keep the CEO's name in the public eye—already do some of the work of CEO agents.

Nor are CEOs who are between assignments good candidates for agents. A CEO agent manages an employed professional's long-term career; the first priority of any job candidate is to focus on securing the next assignment, and an outplacement firm would provide a sharper focus for such an individual. Outplacement services are usually provided to senior executives as part of termination packages and thus do not require personal expense.

Nevertheless, a CEO agent can play an important role, for example, in helping to negotiate the gray area of getting from one assignment to another. Eight months before the expiration of a CEO contract, a board may begin informal discussions about whether to renew the contract and may use a retained search firm to delicately explore alternatives. At the same time, a CEO's own agent can quietly explore new options. When the company and the CEO sit down to renegotiate the employment contract, both sides benefit from a clear sense of market conditions.

A CEO agent may do the legwork to manage an individual's reputation—that intangible asset that defines an executive's individual worth. One time-consuming aspect of reputation management is networking; focused on the demands of the job, an executive may lack the time to keep the network "warm." Consider Phil, a CEO with a network of 850 business contacts. He would reach out to his network only when he needed to find his next assignment; because he didn't otherwise maintain contact or contribute to committees or associations, he became known as a taker rather than as a giver. Phil commissioned a CEO agent to keep his network warm by sending quarterly personal letters, cards, and relevant articles to his contacts; Phil only signed the letters. As a result, the time he spent looking for a new position between assignments shrank from an average of six months to three.

A CEO agent can help, too, to ensure that an individual's public reputation remains strong. According to the public relations firm Burson-Marsteller, 45% of a company's reputation rests on that of its CEO. This percentage has increased almost 14% since 1997. Moreover, 95% of analysts who select stock use CEO reputation as a key decision point.

A CEO agent sometimes acts as a career coach, a person familiar with your industry and company who can serve as a trusted, impartial sounding board and work behind the scenes to help you be more effective on the job. A coach is typically an experienced businessperson who, over the years, has developed a gift for navigating business dynamics and with whom the executive develops a close, one-on-one relationship. If, for example, an executive feels she's been given a cold shoulder by someone in the organization with whom she thought she had a good relationship, a coach can help her backtrack through communications to discern possible sources of contention. Or a coach might help an executive discover ways to sell an idea to various constituents within a company, such as strategizing on how to acquire ownership of other parts of a company while the executive maintains a focus on the core aspects of his or her job.

An agent can also supply an executive with a career management infrastructure—public relations professionals to generate a visibility program, administrative staff to keep a network warm, attorneys specializing in employment contract negotiation, financial planners, and outplacement consultants. An agent might even pair an executive with a theater director to assist with an important "performance."

As with any consulting arrangement, an executive who uses an agent should proceed with caution. Here's how.

Depend on excellent references

CEO agents are difficult to find; good ones work strictly by referral. Other CEOs, or contacts in professions that use agents (sports, publishing, media), may be able to refer you to good ones. A few search firms also provide such services. Don't forget to seek help from associations such as the Young Presidents' Organization or Renaissance Executive Forums.

Ask hard questions

Before entering into a relationship with a CEO agent, hold an exploratory meeting or two during which you ask specific questions about how the agent would help manage your career for the long term. It's also important to have an open discussion about potential conflicts of interest, because the agent may know things about your company that you don't. If, for example, the agent works for a search firm that already has a relationship with your company, it's possible that the agent could be hired to find your successor. To circumvent problems, you and your agent should outline any potential conflicts of interest that either of you can imagine. And if, for any reason, the agent is not on your ethical wavelength, pass.

Understand the arrangement

Don't hire a CEO agent for a onetime transaction. Like your CPA, financial planner, or attorney, your agent is a long-term valued adviser you expect to work with over many years. He or she must be available to you 24/7 to help you with specific work-related and career management issues; it's also wise to include your agent in occasional family discussions about plans and goals. Like professional recruiters and other personal consultants, a CEO agent is hired on retainer, typically charging 5% of the executive's cash compensation, with a $15,000 minimum yearly fee.

Set realistic goals

Work together with your agent to develop six-month and one-year game plans with pragmatic goals. You want to make discernable progress in expanding your visibility, but don't expect miracles. If you are an unknown CEO from a small firm, you probably won't be sitting on the board of a *Fortune* 500 company within three months. Before the annual contract comes up for renewal, meet with your agent to evaluate the year's accomplishments.

Originally published in July–August 2001
Reprint R0107F

Managing Oneself

PETER F. DRUCKER

Executive Summary

THROUGHOUT HISTORY, people had little need to manage their careers—they were born into their station in life or, in the recent past, they relied on their companies to chart their career paths. But times have drastically changed. Today, we must all learn to manage ourselves.

What does that mean? According to Peter Drucker, it means we have to learn to develop ourselves. We have to place ourselves where we can make the greatest contribution to our organizations and communities. And we have to stay mentally alert and engaged during a 50-year working life, which means knowing how and when to change the work that we do.

It may seem obvious that people achieve results by doing what they are good at and by working in ways that fit their abilities. But, Drucker says, very few people actually know—let alone take advantage of—their unique strengths.

73

He challenges each of us to ask ourselves fundamental questions: What are my strengths? How do I perform? What are my values? Where do I belong? What should my contribution be? Don't try to change yourself, cautions Drucker. Instead, concentrate on improving the skills you have and accepting assignments that are tailored to your individual way of working. If you do that, you can transform yourself from an ordinary worker into an outstanding performer.

Successful careers today are not planned out in advance. They develop when people are prepared for opportunities because they have asked themselves those questions, and they have rigorously assessed their unique characteristics. This article challenges readers to take responsibility for managing their futures, both in and out of the office.

HISTORY'S GREAT ACHIEVERS—a Napoleon, a daVinci, a Mozart—have always managed themselves. That, in large measure, is what makes them great achievers. But they are rare exceptions, so unusual both in their talents and their accomplishments as to be considered outside the boundaries of ordinary human existence. Now, most of us, even those of us with modest endowments, will have to learn to manage ourselves. We will have to learn to develop ourselves. We will have to place ourselves where we can make the greatest contribution. And we will have to stay mentally alert and

To stay mentally alert and engaged during a 50-year working life, one must know how and when to change the work one does.

engaged during a 50-year working life, which means knowing how and when to change the work we do.

What Are My Strengths?

Most people think they know what they are good at. They are usually wrong. More often, people know what they are not good at—and even then more people are wrong than right. And yet, a person can perform only from strength. One cannot build performance on weaknesses, let alone on something one cannot do at all.

Throughout history, people had little need to know their strengths. A person was born into a position and a line of work: the peasant's son would also be a peasant; the artisan's daughter, an artisan's wife, and so on. But now people have choices. We need to know our strengths in order to know where we belong.

The only way to discover your strengths is through feedback analysis. Whenever you make a key decision or take a key action, write down what you expect will happen. Nine or 12 months later, compare the actual results with your expectations. I have been practicing this method for 15 to 20 years now, and every time I do it, I am surprised. The feedback analysis showed me, for instance—and to my great surprise—that I have an intuitive understanding of technical people, whether they are engineers or accountants or market researchers. It also showed me that I don't really resonate with generalists.

Feedback analysis is by no means new. It was invented sometime in the fourteenth century by an otherwise totally obscure German theologian and picked up quite independently, some 150 years later, by John Calvin and Ignatius Loyola, each of whom incorporated it into the practice of his followers. In fact, the steadfast focus on performance and results that this habit produces explains why the institutions these two men founded, the Calvinist church and the Jesuit order, came to dominate Europe within 30 years.

Practiced consistently, this simple method will show you within a fairly short period of time, maybe two or three years, where your strengths lie—and this is the most important thing to know. The method will show you what you are doing or failing to do that deprives you of the full benefits of your strengths. It will show you where you are not particularly competent. And finally, it will show you where you have no strengths and cannot perform.

Several implications for action follow from feedback analysis. First and foremost, concentrate on your strengths. Put yourself where your strengths can produce results.

Second, work on improving your strengths. Analysis will rapidly show where you need to improve skills or acquire new ones. It will also show the gaps in your knowledge—and those can usually be filled. Mathematicians are born, but everyone can learn trigonometry.

Third, discover where your intellectual arrogance is causing disabling ignorance and overcome it. Far too many people—especially people with great expertise in one area—are contemptuous of knowledge in other areas or believe that being bright is a substitute for knowledge. First-rate engineers, for instance, tend to take pride in not knowing anything about people. Human beings, they believe, are much too disorderly for the good engineering mind. Human resource professionals, by contrast, often pride themselves on their ignorance of elementary accounting or of quantitative methods altogether. But taking pride in such ignorance is self-defeating. Go to work on acquiring the skills and knowledge you need to fully realize your strengths.

It is equally essential to remedy your bad habits—the things you do or fail to do that inhibit your effectiveness and performance. Such habits will quickly show up in the feedback. For example, a planner may find that his beautiful plans fail because he does not follow through on them. Like so many brilliant people, he believes that ideas move mountains. But bulldozers move mountains; ideas show where the bulldozers should go to work.

It takes far more energy to improve from incompetence to mediocrity than to improve from first-rate performance to excellence.

This planner will have to learn that the work does not stop when the plan is completed. He must find people to carry out the plan and explain it to them. He must adapt and change it as he puts it into action. And finally, he must decide when to stop pushing the plan.

At the same time, feedback will also reveal when the problem is a lack of manners. Manners are the lubricating oil of an organization. It is a law of nature that two moving bodies in contact with each other create friction. This is as true for human beings as it is for inanimate objects. Manners—simple things like saying "please" and "thank you" and knowing a person's name or asking after her family—enable two people to work together whether they like each other or not. Bright people, especially bright young people, often do not understand this. If analysis shows that someone's brilliant work fails again and again as soon as cooperation from others is required, it probably indicates a lack of courtesy—that is, a lack of manners.

Comparing your expectations with your results also indicates what not to do. We all have a vast number of areas in which we have no talent or skill and little chance of becoming even mediocre. In those areas a person—and especially a knowledge worker—should not take on work, jobs, and assignments. One should waste as little effort as possible on improving areas of low competence. It takes far more energy and work to improve from incompetence to mediocrity than it takes to improve from first-rate performance to excellence. And yet most people—especially most teachers and most organizations—concentrate on making incompetent performers into mediocre ones. Energy, resources, and time should go instead to making a competent person into a star performer.

How Do I Perform?

Amazingly few people know *how* they get things done. Indeed, most of us do not even know that different people work and perform differently. Too many people work in ways that are not their ways, and that almost guarantees nonperformance. For knowledge workers, How do I perform? may be an even more important question than What are my strengths?

Like one's strengths, how one performs is unique. It is a matter of personality. Whether personality be a matter of nature or nurture, it surely is formed long before a person goes to work. And *how* a person performs is a given, just as *what* a person is good at or not good at is a given. A person's way of performing can be slightly modified, but it is unlikely to be completely changed—and certainly not easily. Just as people achieve results by doing what they are good at, they also achieve results by working in ways that they best perform. A few common personality traits usually determine how a person performs.

AM I A READER OR A LISTENER?

The first thing to know is whether you are a reader or a listener. Far too few people even know that there are readers and listeners and that people are rarely both. Even fewer know which of the two they themselves are. But some examples will show how damaging such ignorance can be.

When Dwight Eisenhower was commander in chief of the Allied forces in Europe, he was the darling of the press. His press conferences were famous for their style—General Eisenhower showed total command of whatever question he was asked, and he was able to describe a situation and explain a policy in two or three beautifully polished and elegant sentences. Ten years later, the same journalists who had been his admirers held President Eisenhower in open contempt. He never addressed the questions, they complained, but rambled on endlessly about something else. And they constantly ridiculed him for butchering the King's English in incoherent and ungrammatical answers.

Eisenhower apparently did not know that he was a reader, not a listener. When he was commander in chief in Europe, his aides made sure that every question from the press was presented in writing at least half an hour before a conference was to begin. And then Eisenhower was in total command. When he became president, he succeeded two listeners, Franklin D. Roosevelt and Harry Truman. Both men knew themselves to be listeners and both enjoyed free-for-all press conferences. Eisenhower may have felt that he had to do what his two predecessors had done. As a result, he never even heard the questions journalists asked. And Eisenhower is not even an extreme case of a nonlistener.

A few years later, Lyndon Johnson destroyed his presidency, in large measure, by not knowing that he was a listener. His predecessor, John Kennedy, was a reader who had assembled a brilliant group of writers as his assistants, making sure that they wrote to him before discussing their memos in person. Johnson kept these people on his staff—and they kept on writing. He never, apparently, understood one word of what they wrote. Yet as a senator, Johnson had been superb; for parliamentarians have to be, above all, listeners.

Few listeners can be made, or can make themselves, into competent readers—and vice versa. The listener who tries to be a reader will, therefore, suffer the fate of Lyndon Johnson, whereas the reader who tries to be a listener will suffer the fate of Dwight Eisenhower. They will not perform or achieve.

HOW DO I LEARN?

The second thing to know about how one performs is to know how one learns. Many first-class writers—Winston Churchill is but one example—do poorly in school. They tend to remember their schooling as pure torture. Yet few of their classmates remember it the same way. They may not have enjoyed the school very much, but the worst they suffered was boredom. The explanation is that writers do not, as a rule, learn by listening and reading. They learn by writing. Because schools do not allow them to learn this way, they get poor grades.

Schools everywhere are organized on the assumption that there is only one right way to learn and that it is the same way for everybody. But to be forced to learn the way a school teaches is sheer hell for students who learn differently. Indeed, there are probably half a dozen different ways to learn.

There are people, like Churchill, who learn by writing. Some people learn by taking copious notes. Beethoven, for example, left behind an enormous number of sketchbooks, yet he said he never actually looked at them when he composed. Asked why he kept them, he is reported to have replied, "If I don't write it down immediately, I forget it right away. If I put it into a sketchbook, I never forget it and I never have to look it up again." Some people learn by doing. Others learn by hearing themselves talk.

A chief executive I know who converted a small and mediocre family business into the leading company in its industry was one of those people who learn by talking. He was in the habit of calling his entire senior staff into his office once a week and then talking at them for two or three hours. He would raise policy issues and argue three different positions on each one. He rarely asked his associates for comments or questions; he simply needed an audience to hear himself talk. That's how he learned. And although he is a fairly extreme case, learning through talking is by no means an unusual method. Successful trial lawyers learn the same way, as do many medical diagnosticians (and so do I).

Of all the important pieces of self-knowledge, understanding how you learn is the easiest to acquire. When I ask people, "How do you learn?" most of them know the answer. But when I ask, "Do you act on this knowledge?" few answer yes. And yet, acting on this knowledge is the key to performance; or rather, *not* acting on this knowledge condemns one to nonperformance.

How do I perform? and How do I learn? are the first questions to ask. But they are by no means the only ones.

To manage yourself effectively, you also have to ask, Do I work well with people or am I a loner? And if you do work well with people, you then must ask, In what relationship?

Some people work best as subordinates. General George Patton, the great American military hero of World War II, is a prime example. Patton was America's top troop commander. Yet when he was proposed for an independent command, General George Marshall, the U.S. chief of staff—and probably the most successful picker of men in U.S. history—said, "Patton is the best subordinate the American army has ever produced, but he would be the worst commander."

Some people work best as team members. Others work best alone. Some are exceptionally talented as coaches and mentors; others are simply incompetent as mentors.

Another crucial question is, Do I produce results as a decision maker or as an adviser? A great many people perform best as advisers but cannot take the burden and pressure of making the decision. A good many other people, by contrast, need an adviser to force themselves to think; then they can make decisions and act on them with speed, self-confidence, and courage.

This is a reason, by the way, that the number two person in an organization often fails when promoted to the number one position. The top spot requires a decision maker. Strong decision makers often put somebody they trust into the number two spot as their adviser—and in that position the person is outstanding. But in the number one spot, the same person

Do not try to change yourself—you are unlikely to succeed. Work to improve the way you perform.

fails. He or she knows what the decision should be but cannot accept the responsibility of actually making it.

Other important questions to ask include, Do I perform well under stress or do I need a highly structured and predictable environment? Do I work best in a big organization or a small one? Few people work well in all kinds of environments. Again and again, I have seen people who were very successful in large organizations flounder miserably when they moved into smaller ones. And the reverse is equally true.

The conclusion bears repeating: do not try to change yourself—you are unlikely to succeed. But work hard to improve the way you perform. And try not to take on work you cannot perform or will only perform poorly.

What Are My Values?

To be able to manage yourself, you finally have to ask, What are my values? This is not a question of ethics. With respect to ethics, the rules are the same for everybody, and the test is a simple one. I call it the "mirror test."

In the early years of this century, the most highly respected diplomat of all the great powers was the German ambassador in London. He was clearly destined for great things—to become his country's foreign minister, at least, if not its federal chancellor. Yet in 1906 he abruptly resigned rather than preside over a dinner given by the diplomatic corps for Edward VII. The king was a notorious womanizer and made it clear what kind of dinner he wanted. The ambassador is reported to have said, "I refuse to see a pimp in the mirror in the morning when I shave."

That is the mirror test. Ethics requires that you ask yourself, What kind of person do I want to see in the mirror in the morning? What is ethical behavior in one kind of organization or situation is ethical behavior in another. But ethics are only part of a value system—especially of an organization's value system.

To work in an organization whose value system is unacceptable or incompatible with one's own condemns a person both to frustration and to nonperformance.

Consider the experience of a highly successful human resources executive whose company was acquired by a bigger organization. After the acquisition, she was promoted to do the kind of work she did best, which included selecting people for important positions. The executive deeply believed that a company should hire people for such positions from the outside only after exhausting all the inside possibilities. But her new company believed in first looking outside "to bring in fresh blood." There is something to be said for both approaches—in my experience, the proper one is to do some of both. They are, however, fundamentally incompatible—not as policies but as values. They bespeak different views of the relationship between organizations and people; different views of the responsibility of an organization to its people and their development; and different views of a person's most important contribution to an enterprise. After several years of frustration, the executive quit—at considerable financial loss. Her values and the values of the organization simply were not compatible.

Similarly, whether a pharmaceutical company tries to obtain results by making constant, small improvements or by achieving occasional, highly expensive, and risky "breakthroughs" is not primarily an economic question. The results of either strategy may be pretty much the same. At bottom, there is a conflict between a value system that sees the company's contribution in terms of helping physicians do better what they already do and a value system that is oriented toward making scientific discoveries.

Whether a business should be run for short-term results or with a focus on the long term is likewise a question of values. Financial analysts believe that businesses can be run for both simultaneously. Successful businesspeople know better. To be sure, every company has to produce short-term results. But in any conflict between short-term results and long-term growth, each company will determine its own priority. This is not primarily a disagreement about economics. It is fundamentally a value conflict regarding the function of a business and the responsibility of management.

Value conflicts are not limited to business organizations. One of the fastest-growing pastoral churches in the United States measures success by the number of new parishioners. Its leadership believes that what matters is how many newcomers join the congregation. The Good Lord will then minister to their spiritual needs or at least to the needs of a sufficient percentage. Another pastoral, evangelical church believes that what matters is people's spiritual growth. The church eases out newcomers who join but do not enter into its spiritual life.

Again, this is not a matter of numbers. At first glance, it appears that the second church grows more slowly. But it retains a far larger proportion of newcomers than the first one does. Its growth, in other words, is more solid. This is also not a theological problem, or only secondarily so. It is a problem about values. In a public debate, one pastor argued, "Unless you first come to church, you will never find the gate to the Kingdom of Heaven."

"No," answered the other. "Until you first look for the gate to the Kingdom of Heaven, you don't belong in church."

Organizations, like people, have values. To be effective in an organization, a person's values must be compatible with the organization's values. They do not need to be the same, but they must be close enough to coexist. Otherwise, the person will not only be frustrated but also will not produce results.

A person's strengths and the way that person performs rarely conflict; the two are complementary. But there is sometimes a conflict between a person's values and his or her strengths. What one does well—even very well and successfully—may not fit with one's value system. In that case, the work may not appear to be worth devoting one's life to (or even a substantial portion thereof).

If I may, allow me to interject a personal note. Many years ago, I too had to decide between my values and what I was doing successfully. I was doing very well as a young investment banker in London in the mid-1930s, and the work clearly fit my strengths. Yet I did not see myself making a contribution as

What one does well—even very well and successfully—may not fit with one's value system.

an asset manager. People, I realized, were what I valued, and I saw no point in being the richest man in the cemetery. I had no money and no other job prospects. Despite the continuing Depression, I quit—and it was the right thing to do. Values, in other words, are and should be the ultimate test.

Where Do I Belong?

A small number of people know very early where they belong. Mathematicians, musicians, and cooks, for instance, are usually mathematicians, musicians, and cooks by the time they are four or five years old. Physicians usually decide on their careers in their teens, if not earlier. But most people, especially highly gifted people, do not really know where they belong until they are well past their mid-twenties. By that time, however, they should know the answers to the three questions: What are my strengths? How do I perform? and, What are my values? And then they can and should decide where they belong.

Or rather, they should be able to decide where they do *not* belong. The person who has learned that he or she does not perform well in a big organization should have learned to say no to a position in one. The person who has learned that he or she is not a decision maker should have learned to say no to a decision-making assignment. A General Patton (who probably never learned this himself) should have learned to say no to an independent command.

Equally important, knowing the answer to these questions enables a person to say to an opportunity, an offer, or an assignment, "Yes, I will do that. But this is the way I should be doing it. This is the way it should be structured. This is the way the relationships should be. These are the kind of results you should expect from me, and in this time frame, because this is who I am."

Successful careers are not planned. They develop when people are prepared for opportunities because they know their strengths, their method of work, and their values. Knowing where one belongs can transform an ordinary person—hard-working and competent but otherwise mediocre—into an outstanding performer.

What Should I Contribute?

Throughout history, the great majority of people never had to ask the question, What should I contribute? They were told what to contribute, and their tasks were dictated either by the work itself—as it was for the peasant or artisan—or by a master or a mistress, as it was for domestic servants. And until very recently, it was taken for granted that most people were subordinates who did as they were told. Even in the 1950s and 1960s, the new knowledge workers (the so-called organization men) looked to their company's personnel department to plan their careers.

Then in the late 1960s, no one wanted to be told what to do any longer. Young men and women began to ask, What do *I* want to do? And what they heard was that the way to contribute was to "do your own thing." But this solution was as wrong as the organization men's had been. Very few of the people who believed that doing one's own thing would lead to contribution, self-fulfillment, and success achieved any of the three.

But still, there is no return to the old answer of doing what you are told or assigned to do. Knowledge workers in particular have to learn to ask a question that has not been asked before: What *should* my contribution be? To answer it, they must address three distinct elements: What does the situation require? Given my strengths, my way of performing, and my values, how can I make the greatest contribution to what needs to be done? And finally, What results have to be achieved to make a difference?

Consider the experience of a newly appointed hospital administrator. The hospital was big and prestigious, but it had been coasting on its reputation for 30 years. The new administrator decided that his contribution should be to establish a standard of excellence in one important area within two years. He chose to focus on the emergency room, which was big, visible, and sloppy. He decided that every patient who came into the ER had to be seen by a qualified nurse within 60 seconds. Within 12 months, the hospital's emergency room had become a model for all hospitals in the United States, and within another two years, the whole hospital had been transformed.

As this example suggests, it is rarely possible—or even particularly fruitful—to look too far ahead. A plan can usually cover no more than 18 months and still be reasonably clear and specific. So the question in most cases should be, Where and how can I achieve results that will make a difference within the next year and a half? The answer must balance several things. First, the results should be hard to achieve—they should require "stretching," to use the current buzzword. But also, they should be within reach. To aim at results that cannot be achieved—or that can be only under the most unlikely circumstances—is not being ambitious; it is being foolish. Second, the results should be meaningful. They should make a difference. Finally, results should be visible and, if at all possible, measurable. From this will come a course of action: what to do, where and how to start, and what goals and deadlines to set.

Responsibility for Relationships

Very few people work by themselves and achieve results by themselves—a few great artists, a few great scientists, a few great athletes. Most people work with others and are effective with other people. That is true whether they are members of an organization or independently employed. Managing yourself requires taking responsibility for relationships. This has two parts.

The first is to accept the fact that other people are as much individuals as you yourself are. They perversely insist on behaving like human beings. This means that they too have their strengths; they too have their ways of getting things done; they too have their values. To be effective, therefore, you have to know the strengths, the performance modes, and the values of your coworkers.

That sounds obvious, but few people pay attention to it. Typical is the person who was trained to write reports in his or her first assignment because that boss was a reader. Even if the next boss is a listener, the person goes on writing reports that, invariably, produce no results. Invariably the boss will think the employee is stupid, incompetent, and lazy, and he or she will fail. But that could have been avoided if the employee had only looked at the new boss and analyzed how *this* boss performs.

Bosses are neither a title on the organization chart nor a "function." They are individuals and are entitled to do their work in the way they do it best. It is incumbent on the people who work with them to observe them, to find out how they work, and to adapt themselves to what makes their bosses most effective. This, in fact, is the secret of "managing" the boss.

The same holds true for all your coworkers. Each works his or her way, not your way. And each is entitled to work in his or her way. What matters is whether they perform and what their values are. As for how they perform—each is likely to do it differently. The first secret of effectiveness is to understand the people you work with and depend on so that you can make use of their strengths, their ways of working, and their values. Working relationships are as much based on the people as they are on the work.

The second part of relationship responsibility is taking responsibility for communication. Whenever I, or any other consultant, start to work with an organization,

the first thing I hear about are all the personality conflicts. Most of these arise from the fact that people do not
know what other people are doing and how they do their
work, or what contribution the other people are concentrating on and what results they expect. And the reason
they do not know is that they have not asked and therefore have not been told.

This failure to ask reflects human stupidity less than
it reflects human history. Until recently, it was unnecessary to tell any of these things to anybody. In the
medieval city, everyone in a district plied the same trade.
In the countryside, everyone in a valley planted the same
crop as soon as the frost was out of the ground. Even
those few people who did things that were not "common" worked alone, so they did not have to tell anyone
what they were doing.

Today the great majority of people work with others
who have different tasks and responsibilities. The marketing vice president may have come out of sales and
know everything about sales, but she knows nothing
about the things she has never done—pricing, advertising, packaging, and the like. So the people who do these
things must make sure that the marketing vice president
understands what they are trying to do, why they are trying to do it, how they are going to do it, and what results
to expect.

If the marketing vice president does not understand
what these high-grade knowledge specialists are doing, it
is primarily their fault, not hers. They have not educated
her. Conversely, it is the marketing vice president's
responsibility to make sure that all of her coworkers
understand how she looks at marketing: what her goals
are, how she works, and what she expects of herself and
of each one of them.

Even people who understand the importance of taking responsibility for relationships often do not communicate sufficiently with their associates. They are afraid of being thought presumptuous or inquisitive or stupid. They are wrong. Whenever someone goes to his or her associates and says, "This is what I am good at. This is how I work. These are my values. This is the contribution I plan to concentrate on and the results I should be expected to deliver," the response is always, "This is most helpful. But why didn't you tell me earlier?"

And one gets the same reaction—without exception, in my experience—if one continues by asking, "And what do I need to know about your strengths, how you perform, your values, and your proposed contribution?" In fact, knowledge workers should request this of everyone with whom they work, whether as subordinate, superior, colleague, or team member. And again, whenever this is done, the reaction is always, "Thanks for asking me. But why didn't you ask me earlier?"

Organizations are no longer built on force but on trust. The existence of trust between people does not necessarily mean that they like one another. It means that they understand one another. Taking responsibility for relationships is therefore an absolute necessity. It is a duty. Whether one is a member of the organization, a consultant to it, a supplier, or a distributor, one owes that responsibility to all one's coworkers: those whose work one depends on as well as those who depend on one's own work.

The Second Half of Your Life

When work for most people meant manual labor, there was no need to worry about the second half of your life.

You simply kept on doing what you had always done. And if you were lucky enough to survive 40 years of hard work in the mill or on the railroad, you were quite happy to spend the rest of your life doing nothing. Today, however, most work is knowledge work, and knowledge workers are not "finished" after 40 years on the job, they are merely bored.

We hear a great deal of talk about the midlife crisis of the executive. It is mostly boredom. At 45, most executives have reached the peak of their business careers, and they know it. After 20 years of doing very much the same kind of work, they are very good at their jobs. But they are not learning or contributing or deriving challenge and satisfaction from the job. And yet they are still likely to face another 20 if not 25 years of work. That is why managing oneself increasingly leads one to begin a second career.

There are three ways to develop a second career. The first is actually to start one. Often this takes nothing more than moving from one kind of organization to another: the divisional controller in a large corporation, for instance, becomes the controller of a medium-sized hospital. But there are also growing numbers of people who move into different lines of work altogether: the business executive or government official who enters the ministry at 45, for instance; or the midlevel manager who leaves corporate life after 20 years to attend law school and become a small-town attorney.

We will see many more second careers undertaken by people who have achieved modest success in their first jobs. Such people have substantial skills, and they know how to work. They need a community—the house is empty with the children gone—and they need income as well. But above all, they need challenge.

The second way to prepare for the second half of your life is to develop a parallel career. Many people who are very successful in their first careers stay in the work they have been doing, either on a full-time or a part-time or consulting basis. But in addition, they create a parallel job, usually in a nonprofit organization, that takes another ten hours of work a week. They might take over the administration of their church, for instance, or the presidency of the local Girl Scouts Council. They might run the battered women's shelter, work as a children's librarian for the local public library, sit on the school board, and so on.

Finally, there are the social entrepreneurs. These are usually people who have been very successful in their first careers. They love their work, but it no longer challenges them. In many cases they keep on doing what they have been doing all along but spend less and less of their time

There is one prerequisite for managing the second half of your life: you must begin doing so long before you enter it.

on it. They also start another activity, usually a non-profit. My friend Bob Buford, for example, built a very successful television company that he still runs. But he has also founded and built a successful nonprofit organization that works with Protestant churches, and he is building another to teach social entrepreneurs how to manage their own nonprofit ventures while still running their original businesses.

People who manage the second half of their lives may always be a minority. The majority may "retire on the job" and count the years until their actual retirement. But it is this minority, the men and women who see a long working-life expectancy as an opportunity both for themselves and for society, who will become leaders and models.

There is one prerequisite for managing the second half of your life: you must begin long before you enter it. When it first became clear 30 years ago that working-life expectancies were lengthening very fast, many observers (including myself) believed that retired people would increasingly become volunteers for nonprofit institutions. That has not happened. If one does not begin to volunteer before one is 40 or so, one will not volunteer once past 60.

Similarly, all the social entrepreneurs I know began to work in their chosen second enterprise long before they reached their peak in their original business. Consider the example of a successful lawyer, the legal counsel to a large corporation, who has started a venture to establish model schools in his state. He began to do volunteer legal work for the schools when he was around 35. He was elected to the school board at age 40. At age 50, when he had amassed a fortune, he started his own enterprise to build and to run model schools. He is, however, still working nearly full-time as the lead counsel in the company he helped found as a young lawyer.

There is another reason to develop a second major interest, and to develop it early. No one can expect to live very long without experiencing a serious setback in his or her life or work. There is the competent engineer who is passed over for promotion at age 45. There is the competent college professor who realizes at age 42 that she will never get a professorship at a big university, even though she may be fully qualified for it. There are tragedies in one's family life: the breakup of one's marriage or the loss of a child. At such times, a second major interest—not just a hobby—may make all the difference. The engineer, for example, now knows that he has not been very successful in his job. But in his outside activity—as church treasurer, for example—he is a success. One's family may break up, but in that outside activity there is still a community.

In a society in which success has become so terribly important, having options will become increasingly vital. Historically, there was no such thing as "success." The overwhelming majority of people did not expect anything but to stay in their "proper station," as an old English prayer has it. The only mobility was downward mobility.

In a knowledge society, however, we expect everyone to be a success. This is clearly an impossibility. For a great many people, there is at best an absence of failure. Wherever there is success, there has to be failure. And then it is vitally important for the individual, and equally for the individual's family, to have an area in which he or she can contribute, make a difference, and be *somebody*. That means finding a second area—whether in a second career, a parallel career, or a social venture—that offers an opportunity for being a leader, for being respected, for being a success.

The challenges of managing oneself may seem obvious, if not elementary. And the answers may seem self-evident to the point of appearing naïve. But managing oneself requires new and unprecedented things from the individual, and especially from the knowledge worker. In effect, managing oneself demands that each knowledge worker think and behave like a chief executive officer. Further, the shift from manual workers who do as they are told to knowledge workers who have to manage themselves profoundly challenges social structure. Every existing society, even the most individualistic one, takes two things for granted, if only subconsciously: that organizations outlive workers, and that most people stay put.

But today the opposite is true. Knowledge workers outlive organizations, and they are mobile. The need to manage oneself is therefore creating a revolution in human affairs.

Originally published in March–April 1999
Reprint 99204

A Second Career:

The Possible Dream

HARRY LEVINSON

Executive Summary

WHAT MANAGER HASN'T sat at his desk on a gloomy
Monday morning wondering what he was doing there
and asking himself whether he could make it as the skip-
per of a charter boat in the Bahamas or as the operator
of a ski resort in Colorado? Sometimes he dreams of
becoming a lawyer, sometimes simply of writing a book.
Regardless of the dream itself, however, managers need
to satisfy a few conditions, this author says, before they
can be sure that their choice of a second career is a
wise one and not simply a flight from the routine and frustration that is common to all jobs. First managers need to
understand their "ego ideals," their hidden images of
how they would like to be. Then they need to determine
how they prefer to behave in certain situations—whether,
for instance, they prefer risk taking on their own or the
security of groups. Armed with an understanding of their

own visions and behavior patterns, managers are in a position to weigh their career options realistically.

Just two years after his appointment as director of marketing services, 35-year-old Tom Conant started thinking about leaving his job and enrolling in law school. He had fantasies of addressing the bench in an attempt to persuade the judge to side with his position. Tom imagined how it would feel to demolish the opposing lawyer by asking the witness penetrating questions that led inexorably to the conclusion he sought. He couldn't wait to get started.

Tom had joined the company right after business school and in 12 years there had topped one success with another. His marketing acumen, his ability to innovate, do research, and carry through new programs brought the company important new business. In other respects, too, Tom had been a model manager to his superiors and his subordinates. He was marked as a comer. Tom's initial impatience to sink his teeth into new challenges had posed some problems, but as he received new responsibilities, Tom began to relax and seemed to enjoy his work and his colleagues.

When he found himself thinking of a career in law, Tom surprised himself. He had thought that he might be wooed by competitors, but he had never expected to think of abandoning his career. Leo Burns, Tom's predecessor as manager of marketing services and his mentor, hoped to see his protégé follow him to the vice presidency. Tom knew that his resignation would shatter Leo, and that knowledge annoyed him. He didn't want to fight or disappoint Leo.

Anger at Leo slowly mounted. In his fantasy Tom tried to explain to Leo his reasons for leaving, to describe the soul-searching he had done in the last year, but Leo wouldn't listen. He pictured Leo's disappointment turning to irritation. The imaginary drama came to a climax with Leo insisting that Tom leave the company immediately. "Marketing doesn't need you!" Tom imagined Leo shouting. "Just get on with your plans and get out!"

When Tom had these fantasies, he always had second thoughts about making such a move. He had a good career ahead of him. He was a loyal company person, and the company had been good to him. His recent promotion had given him new responsibilities and a reputation in the industry. And he hadn't really been that bored for the last two years.

Yet in calmer moments Tom remembered other managers who had switched careers. An engineer he knew had left a responsible job in product development at the age of 40 to go to law school and was now a patent attorney. He boasted that it was a change he was glad he had made: "I was going to spend the rest of my life putting new faces on old products. Now I can use what I know about engineering to help people who are going to make real changes happen."

Tom reflected also about the many people in the news who were on their second, or even third, careers. California ex-governor Jerry Brown had been a Jesuit seminarian before entering politics; Henry Kissinger had been a professor before becoming a diplomat. Several business school deans had been CEOs, and university presidents have become business executives.

As always, Tom concluded his reverie with a farewell handshake; he was leaving his old friends behind. He

imagined them thinking that they, too, should have
undertaken second careers.

ALMOST EVERYONE AT SOME point thinks of a second career. Many people have good reasons. Tom's law
school fantasy was based in part on a cool assessment of
his own life and the contemporary business situation. He
believed that growing consumer movements would force
the marketing field to change radically in the next
decade. Despite their temporary relaxation, he thought
that federal, state, and local regulations controlling
advertising and promotion would increase. By combin-
ing his marketing experience with a law school education, Tom reasoned he could steal a march on this trend
and build a solid future for himself either as an in-house
counsel or as a consultant.

As the years pass, most people—regardless of their
professions or skills—find their jobs or careers less interesting, stimulating, or rewarding. By midlife, many feel
the need for new and greener occupational fields. They
yearn for opportunities to reassert their independence
and maturity and to express the needs and use the talents of a different stage of life.

Some people feel they are no longer in the running for
advancement, some that their talents and skills are not
being fully used, and some that they have outgrown their
jobs, companies, or disciplines. Others, feeling blocked
by being in the wrong company, industry, or position, are
bored. Some are in over their heads, while others had
merely drifted into their jobs or chosen directions pre-
maturely. One or a combination of these feelings can
make a person hate to go to work in the morning and
can trigger thoughts of a way out.

The realities of contemporary organizational life also stimulate a manager to think about a second career: the competition is stiffer every year. Even to the young manager, the accelerating pace of change makes obsolescence a threat. Rapid technological changes (which demand higher levels of education and training), more differentiated markets, and unpredictable economic circumstances all make it improbable that a manager will have a life-long career in one field or one organization.

By their middle or late 30s, managers usually know how far their careers will take them. By comparing his promotion rate to those of peers, a manager can tell if he has leveled off. If a manager's latest assignment takes him out of the organization's prescribed route to the top, the upward movement probably has ended.

Other factors behind the wish for second careers are the effects aging and growth have on people. Although an intense period of skills training, job rotation, long hours of overtime, and much traveling may have satisfied them when they were younger and just beginning their careers, managers as they get older probably find the pace exhausting and the rewards insufficiently attractive to compensate for the loss of other gratifications.

But the reasons for thinking about a second career are not always positive. Some people want to change because they are always dissatisfied with themselves; some are depressed and angry; some have anxiety about death that induces restlessness; and some have overvalued themselves and believe they are more talented or capable than they really are. Some managers can't tolerate bosses. Others think they should have been CEO a long time ago. Some are unwilling to acquire experience, while others are competing with old classmates. Some are just competing—and not as well as they'd like.

Seeking a new career for these reasons is an exercise in futility. If a manager blames the job, the boss, or the company when the source of his discontent is really himself, his second career is likely to be as disappointing as his first. Therefore a manager, before embarking on choosing a second career, must have an honest picture of himself and understand the changes he probably will go through.

Stages in Adult Development

As middle age approaches, thoughts about a second career intensify.[1] Building on the work of Sigmund Freud, psychoanalyst Erik H. Erikson has outlined three stages of adulthood: intimacy, generativity, and integrity.[2] Each stage has a psychosocial crisis and each has its task.

The first adult stage, intimacy, which lasts from about age 21 to age 35, is the most spontaneously creative period. It is an innovative and productive time. The young adult channels great energies into choosing and launching a career and, usually, into contracting a marriage and establishing a family. The third and final stage, integrity, begins at approximately age 55. Ideally, at this age a person ties together his life experience and comes to terms with his life. At work, he prepares for retirement and reflects on his career.

In between, during the stage of generativity, from about age 35 to age 55, the adult lays the foundations for the next generation. Commonly called the mid-life transition, this is the time of reevaluation. At home, the children are leaving the nest and husbands and wives have to rethink their relationship to each other. At work, the drive to compete and excel is peaking, and executives pay more attention to bringing other, younger managers along.

The transition between intimacy and generativity is, according to Daniel Levinson, the time during which the adult makes his last assertion for independence.[3] Levinson calls this "the BOOM [becoming one's own man] effect." His studies of executives indicate that at about age 37, the adult throws off the guidance or protection of older mentors or managers and takes full charge of himself. Those that are able to make this last stand for independence go on to new heights. They demand more responsibility or start their own companies. Others either don't assert themselves or are rejected when they make demands. The BOOM effect is an impetus for seeking a new career.

In our culture people have opportunities to do many things. In youth they choose one and leave the others behind, but they promise themselves they'll come back to them. Fifteen years out of school, people tend to feel satiated with what they're doing—even if it is something with high status and high pay—and itch to fulfill old promises to themselves. They tend to become restless when circumstances keep them from doing so and become dismayed when they realize that they can't go back and start all over again.

When people are in this stage of life, they need to seek counsel, to talk at length about their reasons, and to listen to others' experiences and perceptions. They also need the support of others who are important to them through this difficult decision-making and transition period. Such assistance can ensure that the manager will make a sound second-career choice rather than flee impulsively from frustration or boredom. It might even result in a wise decision on the part of a promising executive to remain, with renewed enthusiasm, in his organization. A manager who thinks through the issues of a second career also readies himself to help others with the same concerns.

Who Are You?

The most critical factor for people to consider in choosing a gratifying second career is their ego ideal. It can serve as a road map. Central to a person's aspirations, the ego ideal is an idealized image of oneself in the future. It includes the goals people would like to achieve and how they would like to see themselves. At an early age, children identify with parents and other power figures, find out how to please or resist them, and learn to adapt to feeling small and helpless in comparison with them. How they do these things, as well as other unconscious factors, determines how their ego ideals develop. During childhood and adolescence, the young person incorporates rising aspirations built on academic or career achievements into the ego ideal and, as time goes on, also includes successive models, each of which has a more specialized competence.

Throughout life people strive toward their ego ideals, but no one ever achieves it. With successive accomplishments, aspirations rise. But as people feel they are progressing toward their ego ideals, their self-pictures are more rather than less positive. The closer a person gets to the ego ideal, therefore, the better he feels about himself. The greater the gap between one's ego ideal and one's current self-image, the angrier one is at oneself and the more inadequate, guilty, and depressed one feels.

When a career helps satisfy the ego ideal, life and work are rewarding and enjoyable. When a career does not help meet these self-demands, work is a curse. In short, the wish to attain the ego ideal, to like oneself, is the most powerful of motivating forces. Delivery on the promises one makes to oneself is an important aspect of choosing a new direction.

TAPPING INTO THE EGO IDEAL

Because people begin to form their ego ideals in earliest childhood, developing an accurate understanding of them is difficult. A careful review of family history and school and work experiences can go a long way in outlining the needs that are important to the ego ideal. A manager can help the process along by discussing with a listener or a friend answers to the following questions (although this exercise may strike you as off the point, there are very good reasons for carrying it out):

1. What were your father's or father substitute's values? Not what did your father say or do, but what did he stand for? What things were important to him? What was the code he lived by? And then, what were your mother's values?

2. What was the first thing you did that pleased your mother? Small children try hard to please their mothers, who are the most important figures in their lives. Every child's earliest efforts to please mother become ingrained behavior. They are, therefore, a significant part of each person's characteristic way of behaving and have an important influence on subconscious goals. Later, children try to please the father, too.

   (Sometimes, especially for women, it may be the mother's values that are more important and the activities that pleased father that weigh more heavily.)

3. Who were your childhood heroes or heroines? Did you idolize athletes, movie stars, or political figures? What kind of people do you now enjoy reading about or watching on TV? What kind of achievements do you admire?

4. Who are and were your models—relatives, teachers, scoutmasters, preachers, bosses, characters in stories? What did they say or do that made you admire them?

5. When you were able to make choices, what were they? What elective subjects did you take in high school? What major did you pursue in college? What jobs have you accepted? At first glance, these choices may seem to have been random, but they were not. And when you take a retrospective look at them, a pattern emerges.

6. What few experiences in your lifetime have been the most gratifying? Which gave you the greatest pleasure and sense of elation? The pleasure you took in the experience was really the pleasure you took in yourself. What were you doing?

7. Of all the things you've done, at which were you the most successful? What were you doing and how were you doing it?

8. What would you like your epitaph or obituary to say? What would you like to be remembered for? What would you like to leave as a memorial?

The answers to these questions will help managers sketch the outlines of their ego ideals and give them a sense of the main thrust of their lives.

If you still have some doubts about direction after you've talked these questions through, you might take a

battery of psychological tests to complement the defini-
tion of your ego ideal. Many counseling psychologists
provide interest, aptitude, and values inventories as well
as tests of intelligence, reasoning, and other capacities.
They can interpret the test results and advise you about
their significance for your career choice.

How Do You Like to Act?

The next step is to determine the kinds of occupational
activities that fit the way you like to behave, how you like
to do your job or deal with coworkers. The point here is
to determine whether you are temperamentally fit for the
job you're thinking of moving to. For instance, Tom in
the opening vignette had always wanted to take on new
responsibilities and challenges and to act alone taking
risks rather than in a group, where interdependence is
important. If Tom decided to go to law school to become
a consultant working on his own, he would be making a
choice consistent with how he worked best. He would be
choosing an environment in which he would be psychologically comfortable.

In determining how your personality will fit with a
job, a listener's or friend's questions and insights will be
valuable. Explore the following areas:

How do you handle aggressive energy? Do you chan-
nel it into the organization and administration of projects? Are you reluctant to express it? For instance, do
you have difficulty taking people to task or confronting
colleagues or subordinates? How do you react when
someone challenges your opinion?

Channeling aggressive energy into the organization
and administration of projects means that the person
can comfortably take charge and can focus his

achievement effort into organizational achievement rather than personal aggrandizement. A person who is reluctant to express his aggression may have difficulty speaking up at the right time or representing himself adequately or analyzing problems and discussions with other people. Difficulty in taking people to task or confronting colleagues is also a product of reluctance to express aggression and usually reflects a good deal of underlying unconscious guilt.

A person who is unable to take people to task cannot take charge as a manager; and one who is unable to confront others cannot give colleagues or subordinates honest performance appraisals.

How do you handle affection?   Some people prefer to be independent, while others enjoy working closely with people. Do you need constant approval and encouragement or does the quality of your work satisfy you? Can you praise others or do you find it difficult to express positive feelings?

While some people enjoy the affectionate interchange and camaraderie of working closely with others, some people prefer to be independent. The latter may either deny their need for other people's praise, approval, and affection or simply feel more comfortable keeping a distance.

Many managers have great difficulty telling others when they do good work. It is as if any expression of emotion is difficult for them. For some, this is a matter of conscience: they feel like hypocrites for praising work that isn't outstanding. For others, praise may seem to invite a closer relationship with the person being praised or may violate the picture of stoic self-control they want to present.

How do you handle dependency? Do you have trouble making decisions without your manager's OK? Do you work better when you're in charge or in a number 2 position? Do you work as well independently as on a team? Do you have difficulty asking for and using the help of others?

Although most of us fear becoming helplessly dependent on others, in organizations we are necessarily dependent on a lot of other people to get our work done. But some people can't tolerate this aspect of themselves. They need to do everything on their own. It is all right for other people to lean on them, and indeed sometimes they encourage it, but it is not all right for them to lean on other people. Such people disdain others' advice or guidance, even when seeking professional help is appropriate.

On the other hand, some people do well only when they can lean on somebody else's guidance or direction and panic when they don't have that. And while some people may work well by themselves, they may not accept other people's needs to depend on them. Such people will not be good bosses.

Listeners' or friends' special knowledge of a manager's working habits will enable them to be perceptive in questioning the manager in these areas. In addition, the manager should ask others—friends, co-workers, colleagues—to share with him their perceptions of his characteristic behavior. Sometimes they can tell the manager about working habits that he himself is not aware of. For instance, over a period of time friends might have noticed that Tom, from the opening vignette, enjoyed bearing full responsibility and risk for a project and making it work through his own expertise. This information could help Tom choose whether to join a company as in-house counsel or to become an independent consultant. A friend could point out that given his characteristic working style, Tom would probably enjoy the latter better.

In some cases, of course, friends may not be very perceptive or may have their own interests at heart and not be very helpful. At times like these, managers should definitely seek professional help.

Which Way to Go?

Armed with an understanding of his ego ideal and working style, the manager is now ready to weigh options more wisely. He may choose to launch a second career or he may decide to stick with his course in the organization. Whatever his decision, his friends' support and his deeper understanding of himself and his motivation will equip him to attack his chosen career with new dedication and enthusiasm.

Second careers are evolutionary. They stem from some interest that has lain dormant or has been abandoned in favor of another occupation. Asked if he had any idea of what he wanted to do when he left the chairmanship of Dain, Kalman & Quail, an investment banking firm in Minneapolis, for a new vocation, Wheelock Whitney answered, "Yes, really. I thought I'd like to pursue some other things that I cared about." Among these interests was the Johnson Institute, a center studying and treating the chemically dependent. Whitney had become deeply involved in the institute eight years earlier when his wife was undergoing treatment for alcoholism.[4]

Many turn to second careers that extend a previous occupational thrust; they may go into business for them-

selves in fields they already know. By searching the past
for those budding interests that had no chance to flower,
a manager can draw a long list of career options. At the
same time, a manager can eliminate those that are no
longer interesting or pleasurable. In choosing his second
career, William Damroth said he switched from the
chairmanship of Lexington Corporation because "to me
the main thing was that I couldn't continue doing what I
enjoy the most, which is the creative role, the intense
bringing together of all factors, saying, 'It ought to look
like this.' For instance, what I'm doing today is much
more satisfying than the long-range planning you have to
do for a company. Today's satisfaction is immediate."[5]

After eliminating undesirable options, a manager
should investigate what additional training is required
for each of the remaining possibilities and how much he
can afford to invest. To pick up some careers, managers
need to spend years in full-time professional or academic
training; others they can approach through a course of
reading, night school, or correspondence study. By seeing
how the remaining options fit with how he prefers to
behave and by understanding his ego ideal, a manager
can usually narrow the field to one or two general directions. At this point, a manager considering a career
change should again ask a friend or counselor to act as a
sounding board, letting the manager talk through
options and refine his ideas.

Finally, before a manager makes a choice, he should
consider a number of other critical issues:

1. **Family.** Whom do you have responsibility for—a
   mother-in-law, an uncle, a grandfather, a handi-
   capped sister or brother? Do these responsibilities
   limit your options? Do your responsibilities to your

spouse and children impose geographic or financial constraints?

2. **Present job.** If a manager comes to a premature judgment or acts impulsively, he risks leaving his present job thinking that the company left much to be desired. Will your peers and boss see the move as a rejection of the company and of your work together? Feeling abandoned, they might attack you. The possibility of anger and disappointment is especially high when you and your superior have worked closely together and when you respect and admire each other. Furthermore, some people, disappointed that they failed to act when the time was right, will be jealous. They may unload on you their anger with themselves. Are you prepared for these conflicts?

It will help you to think about what it means to lose these peers and mentors. Rather than thinking that you are being disloyal, recognize that people who prepare themselves for a second career are doing the organization as well as themselves a favor by making space for younger, talented managers looking forward to promotion.

3. **Status.** One's status in the community is directly related to one's status at work. Choosing another career may well result in changing one's status. How important is that to you? How important is it that you associate with the same people you have associated with before, that you play golf at the same clubs or take part in the same social activities? Because your spouse and children will also be affected, the family must discuss this issue together. The sacrifices may well be severe.

4. **Rebuilding.** If you're thinking of starting a new business or launching a new career, chances are that you will have to build a clientele. Rarely does a person move from one organization to another and take with him all of his accounts. For example, a lawyer told me that when he and his colleagues left a large firm to start their own, they expected their clients to follow them. Only a small fraction did, and the new firm had to build its clientele from scratch. Anyone starting his own business should expect it to take from two to five years to build a stable of customers.

5. **Freedom v. constraints.** For a mature manager in the BOOM period, the pressure to be autonomous, to do what he wants to do, to be free of commitments to somebody else, is very high. Therefore, in choosing an activity or direction, it is important to choose, insofar as you can, something that allows you maximum freedom to come and go, to do as you wish, while meeting the formal obligations of the role. As William Damroth comments: "My time is my own. I can lie on my back for two hours if I want. Instead of saying, 'This is what I want' and moving toward it, I've said 'This is what I don't like,' and I've eliminated it. I've cut away all the things that make life unhappy for me. I don't have any tension headaches in the mornings."[6]

But one doesn't always achieve freedom so easily. As we go through life we aspire to many things—promotions, new roles, different experiences. And we often ask ourselves, "Who am I to want to do that? What right do I have to seek that goal?" Self-critical feelings often prevent us from moving toward aspirations that we have every right to work toward and achieve.

The issue becomes particularly important with respect to a second career. Because a mature manager recognizes, if he hasn't before, that he has every right to pursue anything he wants to, now is the time to act. Anyone is eligible for any aspiration. One may not achieve it, but one has as much right as anybody else to want it and try for it.

6. **Year-long depression.** I have never seen a person make a significant career shift without experiencing a year-long depression. I don't mean that people are down in the dumps for a year but that they feel loss, ambivalence, and fear that things may not work out. Caught in an ambiguous situation in which they are not yet rooted, they feel detached from their stable routines.

   The longer the manager has been with an organization, the more likely he has come to depend on it; the closer his relationships have been with his colleagues, the greater will be the sense of loss. The more his family has been tied to the organization, the more profound these feelings are likely to be.

7. **Talk.** All change is loss and all loss requires mourning.[7] Even when promoted, one loses the support of colleagues, friends, and known ways of doing things. To dissipate the inevitable sorrow, you have to turn it into words. To detach yourself from old ties and give up old habits, you have to talk about the experience. Feeling that they have to be heroic, some managers, men particularly, either deny that they are having such experiences or grit their teeth and try to plow through them. That way of acting doesn't deal with the depression; it only buries it and makes one vul-

nerable to physiological symptoms and overreactions when traumas occur.

It is important to have somebody to talk to and to be able to talk to that person freely. But even with the most careful and sensitive support from spouse and friends, you may get sidetracked, spin your wheels and get stuck in the mire. If after such talk you are no clearer about your choice, it may be time to consult a professional. The issues and feelings any careful self-appraisal touches on are often too complex to examine or discuss without professional help.

8. **Joint experiences.** Husbands' and wives' careers often separate them. When one member of the marriage makes a career change, new problems having to do with adult development emerge. Early in a marriage the spouses go in different directions, the husband usually to earn a livelihood and the wife usually to bear children. After her childrearing is done, the wife may return to work, but chances are nevertheless that the two spouses will still go in different occupational directions. Their only common interest tends to be the children or family problems.

Usually by the time a person has reached midcareer, the children are out on their own or close to it. The spouses now have to talk to each other. But if they have gone in different directions, they may have trouble communicating. A second career can help spouses reunite. One couple, for example, became interested in antiques. Together they went to antique shows and searched for old glass. When they gave up their old careers, they decided to run an antique store together. What was originally a shared hobby gave the couple financial security while they worked together.

Sometimes a new career threatens an old relationship. One manager was successful and widely respected in his organization. Although unequal to him in status or earning power, his wife also had professional training. When they decided to have children, she left her job to rear them. During those years, he was a supportive helpmate. When she was able, she went to law school and subsequently entered a prestigious law firm. Her status and income now exceed her husband's. He has taken a backseat to her and, with some feelings of embarrassment, carries on some of the household and family maintenance activities that she formerly handled. He speaks of his new situation with mingled pride and shame and is now considering a second career himself.

9. **Open options.** Even if you have exercised great care in choosing a second career, the change won't necessarily work out. Economic vagaries as well as factors that you couldn't foresee may cut your second career short. If you left your old job on a positive note, however, it may be possible to get it back. Many organizations recognize that a manager who has tested himself elsewhere and wants to return is likely to be an even better and more highly motivated employee.

Notes

1. See my article, "On Being a Middle-Aged Manager," HBR July–August 1969, p. 57.

2. Erik H. Erikson, *Childhood and Society*, 2d ed. (New York: Norton, 1963).

3. Daniel Levinson, Charlotte N. Darrow, Edward B. Klein, Maria H. Levinson, and Braxton McKee, *The Seasons of a Man's Life* (New York: Alfred A. Knopf, 1978).

4. See "Don't Call It 'Early Retirement,'" HBR interview with Wheelock Whitney and William G. Damroth, HBR September–October 1975, p. 103.

5. Ibid., p. 113.

6. Ibid., p. 118.

7. See my article, "Easing the Pain of Personal Loss," HBR September–October 1972, p. 80.

Originally published in May–June 1983
Reprint 83307

Five Strategies of Successful Part-Time Work

VIVIEN CORWIN, THOMAS B. LAWRENCE,
AND PETER J. FROST

Executive Summary

NEARLY ONE IN TEN PROFESSIONALS now works
part-time. But all too often, part-time work creates as
many problems as it solves. At best, many part-timers
work more hours than they intended. At worst, they see
their importance to their organization dwindle.

Two generations have wrestled with such arrangements, and today some part-time professionals have
found ways to overcome the challenges, with shining
results. Drawing on two years of research investigating
part-time engineers, financial analysts, IT specialists, and
consultants, the authors present five strategies used by
successful part-timers to make their unique position work
for themselves and their companies.

To begin with, successful part-time professionals take
pains to make their work-life priorities, their schedules, and
their plans for the future transparent to the organization.

Second, they broadcast the business case for their arrangement, being careful to demonstrate that the arrangement has not disrupted the business and may even have a positive impact. Third, they establish routines to protect their time at work and rituals to protect their time at home. Fourth, they cultivate champions in senior management who protect them from skeptics and advocate for their arrangements up and down the ranks. And last, they gently but firmly remind their colleagues that, despite their part-time status, they're still major players in the organization who cannot be ignored.

Taken together, these strategies not only help the part-timer deal with the organization but also make the organization itself more receptive to the possibilities of part-time work.

Most professionals start working part-time to create solutions in their lives. They have young children, want to get MBAs, need to care for aging parents. All too often, though, part-time work creates as many problems as it solves. In the best-case scenario, many part-timers end up working more hours than they intended. In the worst case, they see their importance to their organizations slowly but surely fade away. Now, though, after two generations have wrestled with such arrangements, some part-time professionals have found strategies that are succeeding.

Notice that we say the part-time professionals themselves have found these solutions. For even though most executives would agree, at this point, that part-time work can benefit an organization, it's still up to the part-timers to do most of the heavy lifting. That's true for two reasons. The first is simple: overload. Making a part-time arrangement work takes time, energy, and creativity. Most executives, stressed already with too many day-to-day challenges to list here, see the design and maintenance of part-time work arrangements as just one more hassle. Second, most organizations give executives little in the way of guidelines or policies to help them manage part-time work. So managers have little incentive to get involved. Part-time professionals, then, are on their own in relatively uncharted territory. And, inevitably, map-making falls to the explorers themselves.

For the past two years, we have investigated part-time work as part of a wide-ranging research project examining issues surrounding work-life balance in the United States and Canada. We interviewed 30 part-time professionals in eight organizations, large and small, as well as 27 of their colleagues and managers. Our sample included engineers, financial analysts, information technology specialists, and consultants, among others. About 80% of the part-timers we spoke to were female, largely because so much of part-time work is driven by child care issues, which most often affect women.

Our research revealed strong commonalities in the approaches of successful part-time professionals. Specifically they

- make their work-life priorities, schedules, and (if possible) plans for the future transparent to the organization;

- broadcast the business cases for their arrangements and the nondisruptive—even positive—impact on results;

- establish routines to protect their time at work and rituals to protect their time at home;

- cultivate champions in senior management who not only protect them from skeptics but actively advocate for their arrangements up and down the ranks;

- gently but firmly remind their colleagues that, despite their part-time status, they're still in the game and cannot be ignored.

At first read, some of these strategies may sound familiar—they are, you may be thinking, the same tactics successful full-time professionals use to balance the demands of work and personal life. But look again. The means may be similar, but the end is different. Part-timers use these strategies to generate a protective environment. They're seeking to reduce resentment from full-time colleagues, which can result in marginalization. They're trying to decrease the ambiguity that may confuse their managers, colleagues, families—and sometimes even themselves. And they're aiming to make the organization more comfortable with the concept of part-time work. In the following pages, we'll take a look at these strategies in action. But first, a few words on what our research revealed about the general state of part-time professionals in business today.

Many part-time professionals feel that neither their colleagues nor the organization respects them.

The Part-Timer's Lot

Although nearly 10% of the professional labor force now works part-time, our research found that most part-time jobs are still based on informal agreements. Created on the fly by the part-timers and their bosses, these arrangements are continually adjusted to match the changing demands of work (such as a major client presentation) and home (a child's bout with the flu, say). When organizations do have formal policies about such benefits for part-timers as vacation time and sick pay, they usually serve as rough guidelines only. We found that even in the same company different part-time professionals could work under different terms concerning hours, pay, and benefits. In one department of an organization we studied, for instance, mothers returning from maternity leave were routinely granted part-time positions. In a unit two floors up, such an arrangement was unheard of. "Not even on the docket for discussion," was how one manager put it.

What's more, our research revealed, many part-time professionals feel that neither their colleagues nor the organization respects them. Many part-timers told us they took a lot of jibes about their assumed lack of commitment to work and about their "privileges," such as leaving early. And while most part-timers typically dismissed the razzing as a minor annoyance, they said some discrimination felt very real. Some, for example,

Perceived discrimination makes many part-timers feel defensive about their status, which can put them on the offensive.

were housed in their organization's "low-rent" district where, unlike other professionals, they shared office space with other part-timers. And most lost their eligibility to share in the year-end bonus pool. As one part-time financial analyst put it: "You'd really have to stand on your head, I think, to beat someone for a bonus who is full-time. 'You're part-time,' they say, 'so how could you possibly achieve beyond expectations?' But if I exceed expectations in the days that I'm here, then I should be just as eligible for a bonus as any full-timer."

Most part-timers told us they accepted the consequences of their status as part of the deal. But they also said that sometimes their confidence was eroded, and they questioned whether the arrangement was worth the effort. "Whenever someone questions my position, it sparks a thousand questions in my mind," said a director of client accounts at a worldwide public relations firm. "Am I adding as much value as everybody else? Am I learning the high-tech stuff quickly enough when I am away so often?" Such feelings of inadequacy, some part-timers revealed, can bleed into their personal lives. As the same woman added, "When I'm at work and it seems so hard to pull off a part-time job, I wonder, 'Is my daughter happy when I'm not at home?'"

Perceived discrimination, we found, makes many part-timers feel defensive about their status, which can put them on the offensive. One executive we interviewed didn't even tell her clients that she worked part-time. "I was worried they'd think I wasn't committed or wouldn't get the work done. So if a meeting came up on a Thursday or Friday, I'd be there or I'd send someone for me. I was always accessible by phone and e-mail." Another part-timer told us she had become so defensive about her status that she took steps at work that ultimately undermined the very flexibility she sought from her part-time arrangement. If special training was offered on her day off, for instance, she'd still attend, or if a child was ill on the day of a big meeting, she'd still send him to school. When a big project was due, she'd work nights and weekends. "It's worth it," she told us, "so the organization knows I am as committed to them as they are to me." (Incidentally, this woman was not part of the group of part-time professionals from which we drew our conclusions about successful strategies.)

These stories are extreme cases. But nearly all of our respondents admitted that work regularly crept into the private areas of their lives. Study participants typically encouraged emergency calls at home, attended important meetings during their scheduled time off, and used technology to stay in touch with work. True, these practices were usually described as exceptions, but they happened often enough to suggest that the boundary between work and home is difficult to protect.

Fortunately, the picture for part-time professionals is not entirely grim—far from it. Let's take a look at the strategies that part-timers have devised to make their unique status a success.

Strategy 1

Successful part-time professionals make their work-life priorities, schedules, and (if possible) plans for the future transparent to the organization.

Although the majority of part-time professionals are women seeking more time with their children, the reasons for alternative work arrangements vary as much as the professionals themselves. Some individuals in our study worked part-time in order to go back to school; others were caring for aging parents. It's precisely because part-time professionals have such diverse motives that they need to be frank about their priorities. Such clarity paves the way for the open, honest communication on which part-time work thrives.

Would-be part-timers cannot assume their employers will automatically divine the reasons for moving to part-time status. Many bosses will shy away from knowing anything about an employee's private life in a well-intentioned effort to respect her privacy. But not knowing the part-timer's "life story," so to speak, has its consequences. A number of managers and coworkers in our study, for instance, were remarkably reluctant to contact part-timers at home. Ironically, this usually added to the part-time professionals' workloads: once back in the office, they had to correct festering problems that could easily have been resolved through a quick call.

The most successful part-timers in our study avoided such land mines by clearly explaining to bosses and colleagues why they were working part-time, what kinds of intrusions on their home time were acceptable, and even how long they planned to stay part-time. In short, they were explicit about their priorities. One successful part-time professional, for instance, announced in writing to a wide swath of her coworkers that she was working part-time so that she could be with her young daughter in the afternoons but that she still considered her work central to her life and looked forward to returning to working full-time in 18 months. Another woman made her priorities explicit, saying she was working 20 hours a week because she had entered an eight- to ten-year time in her life when her family came first, period. These two approaches to part-time work imply two very different relationships between the part-timer and the organization. Both can succeed, however, because they are perfectly clear.

Our research showed that the more explicit employees can be about their priorities, the greater the chances are that they can sit down with their managers and shape mutually satisfying working arrangements. When part-timers clearly articulate their needs, employers can work out what degree of commitment to expect, not just at the beginning but throughout the arrangement. Consider a systems analyst for a major oil company. When he first approached his managers, he was blunt about his personal priorities: "I told them I wanted to participate more in the rearing of my children and I wanted to start my MBA. I explained that I wanted to work part-time—and, for me, that was non-negotiable." This tough stance gave both the analyst and his management a clear understanding of what he needed as they worked together to design a feasible solution. They ended up forging an unusually favorable part-time deal for two years. The analyst would work two days a week, and the organization agreed that he would not be required to stretch his work commitments without ample notice. The analyst's project manager agreed to take up some of the slack when he, the analyst, was out of the office. The manager was prepared to step in, she explained, because the analyst had a stellar track record, and she was confident that he was making the project's success a priority.

Like the systems analyst, all the successful part-timers in our study were individuals who had formerly done outstanding full-time work. Indeed, part-time work is not a viable route for anyone who hasn't already demonstrated superiority in a traditional setting. Successful part-timers know the company ropes. They've learned the organization's rules, they've mastered those rules, and now they're ready to change them. Of course, not every part-time professional can—or wants to—set down such unequivocal terms. But making their new priorities transparent to the organization will help professionals outperform in their part-time positions just as they did when they were full-time.

Strategy 2

Successful part-time professionals broadcast the business cases for their arrangements and the nondisruptive—even positive—impact on results.

Simply put, the main reason most bosses and colleagues object to part-time work is that they suspect it will disrupt the business. They're afraid work won't get done on time or that other people, already at full capacity, will need to pick up the part-timer's unwanted assignments. These worries are legitimate. That's why the successful part-timers in our study did not ignore or gloss over them. They addressed them head on.

First, many part-timers help their organizations to see that the arrangement makes more sense than a complete departure. This always needs to be handled with subtlety, for obvious reasons. No one likes to hear, "Consider yourself lucky you've got me at all!" But there is really no reason for being so direct. Bosses know that part-timers have successful track records—as well as insider knowledge, existing relationships, and technical expertise. They need only a slight nudge to remind them what would happen if a part-timer were to move to the competition.

Second, successful part-timers publicize the business cases for their arrangements by demonstrating that the work is still getting done, well and on time. One fundamental way they do this is by building strong alliances with their colleagues. In fact, the successful part-timers in our study involved their coworkers as much as possible in the initial transition from full-time status. One customer service engineer, for example, discussed the shift to part-time with all the members of her team before she raised the idea formally: "Politically, it would have been impossible for my boss to turn me down."

Nevertheless, a part-time arrangement will in fact change the way work gets done. In consulting businesses, for instance, with their high premium on service, the part-timer will not always be available to the client. Extra work will inevitably spill over to coworkers, causing friction among even the best-oiled groups. Therefore, successful part-timers go to great lengths to reassure colleagues that they are not simply entitled to special privileges. At times, this means reminding people that although they work less, part-timers also earn less.

At all times, it is important for part-timers to frame the extra responsibilities that fall on coworkers and subordinates as opportunities. Thus, the successful part-timer is careful to delegate work around her colleagues' development needs by, for instance, having a compatriot who needs to work on facilitation skills lead a meeting the part-timer is not going to. In this way, she can help coworkers benefit from the extra work they're given.

Finally, creating a business case for a reduced schedule often requires part-timers to redesign their work so that they, in effect, end up doing the same amount of work but more efficiently. Those part-timers we studied who were able to achieve this heightened productivity were almost always highly motivated, committed self-starters. Consider a customer service manager for a phone company. She took the job on a half-time basis. Her predecessor had held the same job full-time. The work content didn't diminish at all. In fact, it increased. But the service manager now gets the job done in half the time.

This is often the case. All the successful part-timers in our study had rich anecdotal evidence of their ability to squeeze more work into less time. And the managers interviewed in our study agreed. Said a manager of two engineers who worked part-time: "We probably get as much productivity out of our part-time professionals as we do from some of the employees who are here five days a week."

Strategy 3

Successful part-time professionals establish routines to protect their time at work and rituals to protect their time at home.

Our study showed that successful part-timers approach the pace and flow of their work in a wide variety of ways. One financial analyst at an electric utility, for instance, spread out her days in the office, working Mondays, Wednesdays, and Fridays. The benefit, she claimed, was that she stayed in touch with the work situation, and her mind was less likely to drop out of work mode. But another professional in our study—an account executive at a major oil company—stayed focused by doing just the reverse. She worked Monday through Wednesday every week.

No matter what their schedules, successful part-time professionals establish routines that are transparent to their colleagues and bosses and help them separate work and home in their own minds. From the company's perspective, we found, the nature of the routine selected is much less important than its sheer regularity. Similarly, the successful part-timers in our study demarcated home and work with personalized rituals, which again served to clarify where they were and when.

But successful part-timers don't stop at organizing their own work. They pay attention to how the work is flowing when they're not around, as well. One systems analyst, for example, described how colleagues would let work slide until Thursday because they knew she wouldn't be coming into the office until then. This led her to establish monitoring routines in which she hounded people virtually on her days off. Every day or so, she left voice-mail and e-mail messages ensuring that the flow of work continued smoothly. Communication routines let her know when she needed to put her foot down. They also let her colleagues know that she was never very far away.

Routines, of course, are easier praised than actually practiced. Business is always in flux; emergencies happen. Meetings come up unexpectedly, often throwing the airtight schedule of the part-timer into disarray. That's why in establishing their routines part-timers need to set some judicious rules about their participation in meetings.

Now it might seem logical for part-timers to attend all the meetings they can when they're in the office: after all, missing meetings on days off is already something of a political statement. It implies, "I don't care about this organization's pecking order. I come and go as I please." Few part-timers deliberately want to make such a statement. But our research suggests that a surprising number of successful part-time professionals miss meetings even on days when they are in the office, as part of their standard routine. One systems analyst we interviewed was emphatic about the need to protect her work time: "I tend to avoid meetings like the plague because they're a waste of time." In fact, successful part-timers draw on their insider knowledge of organizational routines to make tough judgment calls about which meetings they can safely ignore and which they need to attend.

Now for rituals, which are important, we found, because they fortify the boundaries between work and home that part-timers need to sustain their delicate arrangements. So one part-timer described how every week, come what may, he coaches his daughter's basketball team and attends all the games. Another part-timer who doesn't work on Fridays deliberately leaves her laptop at work on Thursday nights. Still another professional fills up her home time with piano lessons and sewing classes. "I'm not a schedule person," she said, "but I've consciously scheduled my time."

Unlike routines, rituals often have a symbolic component in that they force part-time professionals to invest not only time but also emotion into something. We heard from a number of part-timers who regularly participated in a range of community groups, from gardening clubs to dance troupes to Bible study groups. These activities demand a commitment from part-timers to people and places that are unrelated to work—and often unrelated to children and home. These rituals that part-time professionals erect in their lives are among the most effective because they genuinely break connections with the known world and forge new ties.

Strategy 4

Successful part-time professionals cultivate champions in senior management who not only protect them from skeptics but actively advocate for their arrangements up and down the ranks.

The idiosyncratic nature of part-time work makes each part-time professional an organizational innovator, with all the risks that innovation implies. And, as with any risky investment, the part-time position often requires a sponsor, someone who can influence the way the company views the shift to part-time work. Consider the experience of an IT specialist working at a gas pipeline company. She was stressed out, losing weight, and finding it impossible to do her job while raising three children. Although her coworkers were compassionate, they couldn't see how a part-time arrangement could work out without harming them. Without some senior-level support, the IT specialist wasn't going to get any-where. But she fought hard for a change in status. She talked to a wide range of potential champions until finally she found a sympathetic ear. Although he didn't have an immediate solution, he was able to find another person looking to go part-time. Eventually, he arranged a job they could share.

All the successful part-timers in our study had champions in senior management who helped them overcome obstacles that would otherwise have caused them to fail. That was particularly true for women coming back from maternity leave who assumed (mistakenly) that there would automatically be workable part-time jobs waiting for them when they got back. Champions also play important roles after the work arrangements have been settled. Often, they run interference with clients, managers, and colleagues who may believe that part-timers aren't holding up their end of the bargain. Champions often have to intervene with clients to protect part-timers from excessive customer demands. But champions also make sure that managers are aware of part-timers' contributions and potential so that companies consider these professionals for promotions, bonuses, and choice assignments.

Finally, champions keep part-timers in the loop. They make sure that the part-timer knows what's going on behind the scenes. One champion, for instance, warned his part-time systems analyst that he hadn't been visible enough in the past couple months: "I think you need to go and talk to your team," the champion said. "A few people are reportedly unhappy that you've been so aloof lately." Over time, a good champion accepts some responsibility for making the part-time position work, becoming the part-timer's mentor and protector.

There's no single profile of the ideal champion, but our study found them all to be highly networked change agents—individuals accustomed to using their charisma to influence people at every level of the company. They also tended to be sympathetic to the plight of part-timers because their own spouses or partners were also trying to navigate the challenges of part-time work. Their support of part-time work was, in other words, often quite personal.

Strategy 5

Successful part-time professionals gently but firmly remind their colleagues that, despite their part-time status, they're still in the game and cannot be ignored.

In addition to needing a powerful champion, the part-timer must also build a strong network of allies in the organization to avoid becoming marginalized. Unfortunately, because of their intensified work schedules, part-time professionals often focus on work to the exclusion of making small talk in the corridors. As one consultant in a public relations firm put it: "I want to stay out of politics and all the stuff that floats around. I want to focus on my job. The rest bogs me down."

Our research suggests that such behavior ultimately hurts a professional who already spends so much time away from the office. Office gossip, in particular, helps the part-timer stay tied in. In fact, staying connected turned out to be so important in our study that we've taken to defining a successful part-time professional as someone who can squander time productively at work. Consider Yvonne, the part-time financial analyst at the electric utility. She said that maintaining her social networks was one of the biggest factors in her success. "Some people say I only come in for lunch!" she said. "And I do have a lunch date almost every day that I come in. But that's how I get the informal information I need to make the part-time position work."

Every successful part-timer in our study had some trick for staying visible in the organization despite the many hours spent away from work.

In addition to tuning in to gossip in these informal conversations, part-timers constantly need to emphasize what they have in common with their full-time colleagues. By saying, "I'm not so different from you," part-timers can reassure coworkers that they're not getting a special deal. Take the case of a senior auditor at the gas pipeline company, who successfully defused a coworker's envy over her attendance at a training meeting. "He came up to me and said, 'What are you doing here? Do you get paid to be trained?' 'Yes,' I gently replied. 'Every employee does.'"

The real challenge for part-timers is making their presence felt when they are so often out of the office. Interestingly, every successful part-timer in our study had some trick for staying visible in the organization despite the many hours spent away from work. Some part-timers, for example, sent voice-mails on days when they weren't in the office. Some managed their own projects—and championed others' besides—to show they were very involved. One part-timer devised an elaborate series of meetings, planned and announced long in advance. "Just in case anyone has any doubts," she said defiantly. "I'm around and intend to be for a long time." Successful part-timers show that they cannot be ignored.

BEGUN MORE THAN 20 YEARS AGO, part-time professional work is an experiment that has met with mixed results. In most cases, the arrangement is an attempt to give a woman more time to raise her family. But it is not necessarily a panacea for striking a balance between work and life. Many part-timers are forced to work longer hours than they contracted for, and many suffer under the second-class status of part-time work. At the same time, part-time work makes organizations uncomfortable. It raises obvious questions about who will pick up the slack. And it raises more fundamental questions about the very nature of professional work itself. What exactly is a professional being paid for? Time or output? When limits are placed on time and pay, how should that fairly be reflected in the work?

Successful part-timers face such difficulties head on. The five strategies we've distilled from the experience of the successful part-timers work together to overcome these challenges. They not only help the part-timer deal with the organization but also make the organization itself more receptive to the possibilities of part-time work.

Counsel for Managers

MANY MANAGERS ARE NOT enthusiastic about supporting part-time professionals. Indeed, part-time work may not suit your company. Even in the best of situations, the transition from full-time to part-time is difficult, and managers need to carefully evaluate potential part-timers. As a manager in a telecommunications company put it, "It's a hard road for me and for the employee. I wouldn't do this for just anyone." In fact, our research shows that the odds of success go way up if managers look for people who have already demonstrated success in a full-time position. In addition, this individual should fiercely want a part-time position and have a palpable reason for making it work.

Adding part-time professionals to the staff definitely complicates a manager's life. Suddenly you are called on to determine what constitutes a "fair" schedule and workload. Don't count on guidelines—there aren't any. And it doesn't end there. How are you going to evaluate your part-timer when it comes to bonuses? Is it possible to assess performance for the entire staff in a uniform way, or will the part-timer require more sensitive arrangements? In addition to these concerns, managers also have to work closely with all the people the part-timer interacts with. Sure, it's up to the part-timer to build networks with colleagues and clients, but managers constantly need to take the temperature of the experiment, especially in the early stages. How is the arrangement going for the client? For coworkers? What's life like for the part-timer? The answers to these questions may not be as straightforward as they might seem. As one oil company manager discovered: "I found out quite by chance that our part-timer was demoralized by her workload. The arrangement almost collapsed, and we came close to losing a good employee."

Once you decide to take on a part-timer, moreover, you need to recognize up front that there are limits to the arrangement. Our research suggests, for example, that part-timers are not best placed in situations that demand a lot of face-to-face time—that is, when the politics of a project are precarious or when project members require a lot of hand-holding and cajoling. There are other restrictions. "Sometimes you just don't want a part-timer in charge of a new or complex project," the manager of one company put it bluntly.

Every part-time arrangement is unique. Having one bad—or good—experience doesn't guarantee that you'll have another like it. Every arrangement needs to be set up and managed on its own merits. Who is the particular employee? What is the specific task that needs to be done? In each case, the managerial challenge is to figure out what makes for a good part-timer—and what makes for good part-time work.

Originally published in July–August 2001
Reprint R0107J

Managing Your Boss

JOHN J. GABARRO AND JOHN P. KOTTER

Executive Summary

"WHEN WE FIRST WROTE THIS ARTICLE late in 1979, the idea of managing your boss was an illegitimate notion," recalls author John Gabarro. "Except for one article that Peter Drucker had written about 20 years earlier, there was nothing in management literature on the idea."

At the time, Gabarro and coauthor John Kotter were working together on organizational behavior at Harvard Business School. Doing very different kinds of field research on effective managers, both found that managing one's own boss was crucial to success. In fact, effective managers handled lateral, upward, and downward relationships equally well.

As Gabarro and Kotter developed more data, the value of boss-managing became more and more clear to them. Their focus on what works, or effective behavior,

141

led them to an insight that still cuts through the folklore. Forget ambition. Forget promotion. Forget raises. Just think of the job and how to be effective in it. How do you get the resources you need—the information, the advice, even the permission? The answers always point toward whoever has the power, the leverage, that is, the boss. To fail to make that relationship one of mutual respect and understanding is to miss a major factor of effectiveness.

When they realized they were on to something basic, Gabarro and Kotter took their notes to an HBR editor, who immediately agreed to work with them on this land-mark article. Published in January–February 1980, "Managing Your Boss" is one of HBR's best-selling reprints.

To MANY PEOPLE, the phrase *managing your boss* may sound unusual or suspicious. Because of the traditional top-down emphasis in most organizations, it is not obvious why you need to manage relationships upward—unless, of course, you would do so for personal or political reasons. But we are not referring to political maneuvering or to apple polishing. We are using the term to mean the process of consciously working with your superior to obtain the best possible results for you, your boss, and the company.

Recent studies suggest that effective managers take time and effort to manage not only relationships with their subordinates but also those with their bosses. These studies also show that this essential aspect of management is sometimes ignored by otherwise talented and aggressive managers. Indeed, some managers who actively and effectively supervise subordinates, products, markets, and technologies assume an almost passively reactive stance vis-à-vis their bosses. Such a stance almost always hurts them and their companies.

If you doubt the importance of managing your relationship with your boss or how difficult it is to do so effectively, consider for a moment the following sad but telling story:

Frank Gibbons was an acknowledged manufacturing genius in his industry and, by any profitability standard, a very effective executive. In 1973, his strengths propelled him into the position of vice president of manufacturing for the second largest and most profitable company in its industry. Gibbons was not, however, a good manager of people. He knew this, as did others in his company and his industry. Recognizing this weakness, the president made sure that those who reported to Gibbons were good at working with people and could compensate for his limitations. The arrangement worked well.

Successful managers develop relationships with everyone they depend on—including the boss.

In 1975, Philip Bonnevie was promoted into a position reporting to Gibbons. In keeping with the previous pattern, the president selected Bonnevie because he had an excellent track record and a reputation for being good with people. In making that selection, however, the president neglected to notice that, in his rapid rise through the organization, Bonnevie had always had good-to-excellent bosses. He had never been forced to manage a relationship with a difficult boss. In retrospect, Bonnevie admits he had never thought that managing his boss was a part of his job.

Fourteen months after he started working for Gibbons, Bonnevie was fired. During that same quarter, the company reported a net loss for the first time in seven

years. Many of those who were close to these events say
that they don't really understand what happened. This
much is known, however: while the company was bringing out a major new product—a process that required
sales, engineering, and manufacturing groups to coordi-
nate decisions very carefully—a whole series of misunderstandings and bad feelings developed between Gibbons and Bonnevie.

For example, Bonnevie claims Gibbons was aware of
and had accepted Bonnevie's decision to use a new type
of machinery to make the new product; Gibbons swears
he did not. Furthermore, Gibbons claims he made it clear
to Bonnevie that introduction of the product was too
important to the company in the short run to take any
major risks.

As a result of such misunderstandings, planning went
awry: a new manufacturing plant was built that could
not produce the new product designed by engineering, in
the volume desired by sales, at a cost agreed on by the
executive committee. Gibbons blamed Bonnevie for the
mistake. Bonnevie blamed Gibbons.

Of course, one could argue that the problem here was
caused by Gibbons's inability to manage his subordinates. But one can make just as strong a case that the
problem was related to Bonnevie's inability to manage
his boss. Remember, Gibbons was not having difficulty
with any other subordinates. Moreover, given the personal price paid by Bonnevie (being fired and having his
reputation within the industry severely tarnished), there
was little consolation in saying the problem was that
Gibbons was poor at managing subordinates. Everyone
already knew that.

We believe that the situation could have turned out
differently had Bonnevie been more adept at under-

standing Gibbons and at managing his relationship with him. In this case, an inability to manage upward was unusually costly. The company lost $2 million to $5 million, and Bonnevie's career was, at least temporarily, disrupted. Many less costly cases similar to this probably occur regularly in all major corporations, and the cumulative effect can be very destructive.

Misreading the Boss-Subordinate Relationship

People often dismiss stories like the one we just related as being merely cases of personality conflict. Because two people can on occasion be psychologically or temperamentally incapable of working together, this can be an apt description. But more often, we have found, a personality conflict is only a part of the problem—sometimes a very small part.

Bonnevie did not just have a different personality from Gibbons, he also made or had unrealistic assumptions and expectations about the very nature of boss-subordinate relationships. Specifically, he did not recognize that his relationship to Gibbons involved *mutual dependence* between two *fallible* human beings. Failing to recognize this, a manager typically either avoids trying to manage his or her relationship with a boss or manages it ineffectively.

Bosses can link managers to the rest of the organization, help them set priorities, and secure the resources they need.

Some people behave as if their bosses were not very dependent on them. They fail to see how much the boss needs their help and cooperation to do his or her job effectively. These people refuse to acknowledge that the boss can be severely hurt by their actions and needs cooperation, dependability, and honesty from them.

Some people see themselves as not very dependent on their bosses. They gloss over how much help and information they need from the boss in order to perform their own jobs well. This superficial view is particularly damaging when a manager's job and decisions affect other parts of the organization, as was the case in Bonnevie's situation. A manager's immediate boss can play a critical role in linking the manager to the rest of the organization, making sure the manager's priorities are consistent with organizational needs, and in securing the resources the manager needs to perform well. Yet some managers need to see themselves as practically self-sufficient, as not needing the critical information and resources a boss can supply.

Many managers, like Bonnevie, assume that the boss will magically know what information or help their subordinates need and provide it to them. Certainly, some bosses do an excellent job of caring for their subordinates in this way, but for a manager to expect that from all bosses is dangerously unrealistic. A more reasonable expectation for managers to have is that modest help will be forthcoming. After all, bosses are only human. Most really effective managers accept this fact and assume primary responsibility for their own careers and development. They make a point of seeking the information and help they need to do a job instead of waiting for their bosses to provide it.

In light of the foregoing, it seems to us that managing a situation of mutual dependence among fallible human beings requires the following:

1. That you have a good understanding of the other person and yourself, especially regarding strengths, weaknesses, work styles, and needs.

2. That you use this information to develop and manage a healthy working relationship—one that is compatible with both people's work styles and assets, is characterized by mutual expectations, and meets the most critical needs of the other person. This combination is essentially what we have found highly effective managers doing.

Understanding the Boss

Managing your boss requires that you gain an understanding of the boss and his or her context, as well as your own situation. All managers do this to some degree, but many are not thorough enough.

At a minimum, you need to appreciate your boss's goals and pressures, his or her strengths and weaknesses. What are your boss's organizational and personal objectives, and what are his or her pressures, especially those from his or her own boss and others at the same level? What are your boss's long suits and blind spots? What is the preferred style of working? Does your boss like to get information through memos, formal meetings, or phone calls? Does he or she thrive on conflict or try to minimize it?

Without this information, a manager is flying blind when dealing with the boss, and unnecessary conflicts, misunderstandings, and problems are inevitable.

In one situation we studied, a top-notch marketing manager with a superior performance record was hired into a company as a vice president "to straighten out the marketing and sales problems." The company, which was having financial difficulties, had recently been acquired by a larger corporation. The president was eager to turn it around and gave the new marketing vice president free rein—at least initially. Based on his previous experience, the new vice president correctly diagnosed that greater market share was needed for the company and that strong product management was required to bring that about. Following that logic, he made a number of pricing decisions that were aimed at increasing high-volume business.

When margins declined and the financial situation did not improve, however, the president increased pressure on the new vice president. Believing that the situation would eventually correct itself as the company gained back market share, the vice president resisted the pressure.

When by the second quarter, margins and profits had still failed to improve, the president took direct control over all pricing decisions and put all items on a set level of margin, regardless of volume. The new vice president began to find himself shut out by the president, and their relationship deteriorated. In fact, the vice president found the president's behavior bizarre. Unfortunately, the president's new pricing scheme also failed to increase margins, and by the fourth quarter, both the president and the vice president were fired.

What the new vice president had not known until it was too late was that improving marketing and sales had been only *one* of the president's goals. His most immediate goal had been to make the company more profitable—quickly.

Nor had the new vice president known that his boss was invested in this short-term priority for personal as well as business reasons. The president had been a strong advocate of the acquisition within the parent company, and his personal credibility was at stake.

The vice president made three basic errors. He took information supplied to him at face value, he made assumptions in areas where he had no information, and—what was most damaging—he never actively tried to clarify what his boss's objectives were. As a result, he ended up taking actions that were actually at odds with the president's priorities and objectives.

Managers who work effectively with their bosses do not behave this way. They seek out information about the boss's goals and problems and pressures. They are alert for opportunities to question the boss and others around him or her to test their assumptions. They pay attention to clues in the boss's behavior. Although it is imperative that they do this especially when they begin working with a new boss, effective managers also do this on an ongoing basis because they recognize that priorities and concerns change.

Being sensitive to a boss's work style can be crucial, especially when the boss is new. For example, a new president who was organized and formal in his approach replaced a man who was informal and intuitive. The new president worked best when he had written reports. He also preferred formal meetings with set agendas.

One of his division managers realized this need and worked with the new president to identify the kinds and frequency of information and reports that the president wanted. This manager also made a point of sending background information and brief agendas ahead of time for their discussions. He found that with this type of preparation their meetings were very useful. Another interesting result was, he found that with adequate preparation his new boss was even more effective at brainstorming problems than his more informal and intuitive predecessor had been.

In contrast, another division manager never fully understood how the new boss's work style differed from that of his predecessor. To the degree that he did sense it, he experienced it as too much control. As a result, he seldom sent the new president the background information he needed, and the president never felt fully prepared for meetings with the manager. In fact, the president spent much of this time when they met trying to get information that he felt he should have had earlier. The boss experienced these meetings as frustrating and inefficient, and the subordinate often found himself thrown off guard by the questions that the president asked. Ultimately, this division manager resigned.

The difference between the two division managers just described was not so much one of ability or even adaptability. Rather, one of the men was more sensitive to his boss's work style than the other and to the implications of his boss's needs.

Understanding Yourself

The boss is only one-half of the relationship. You are the other half, as well as the part over which you have more direct control. Developing an effective working relationship requires, then, that you know your own needs, strengths and weaknesses, and personal style.

You are not going to change either your basic personality structure or that of your boss. But you can become aware of what it is about you that impedes or facilitates working with your boss and, with that awareness, take actions that make the relationship more effective.

For example, in one case we observed, a manager and his superior ran into problems whenever they disagreed. The boss's typical response was to harden his position and overstate it. The manager's reaction was then to raise the ante and intensify the forcefulness of his argument. In doing this, he channeled his anger into sharpening his attacks on the logical fallacies he saw in his boss's assumptions. His boss in turn would become even more adamant about holding his original position. Predictably, this escalating cycle resulted in the subordinate avoiding whenever possible any topic of potential conflict with his boss.

In discussing this problem with his peers, the manager discovered that his reaction to the boss was typical of how he generally reacted to counterarguments—but with a difference. His response would overwhelm his peers but not his boss. Because his attempts to discuss this problem with his boss were unsuccessful, he concluded that the only way to change the situation was to deal with his own instinctive reactions. Whenever the two reached an impasse, he would check his own impatience and suggest that they break up and think about it before getting together again. Usually when they renewed their discussion, they had digested their differences and were more able to work them through.

Gaining this level of self-awareness and acting on it are difficult but not impossible. For example, by reflecting over his past experiences, a young manager learned that he was not very good at dealing with difficult and emotional issues where people were involved. Because he disliked those issues and realized that his instinctive responses to them were seldom very good, he developed a habit of touching base with his boss whenever such a problem arose. Their discussions always surfaced ideas and approaches the manager had not considered. In many cases, they also identified specific actions the boss could take to help.

Although a superior-subordinate relationship is one of mutual dependence, it is also one in which the subordinate is typically more dependent on the boss than the other way around. This dependence inevitably results in the subordinate feeling a certain degree of frustration, sometimes anger, when his actions or options are constrained by his boss's decisions. This is a normal part of life and occurs in the best of relationships. The way in which a manager handles these frustrations largely depends on his or her predisposition toward dependence on authority figures.

Some people's instinctive reaction under these circumstances is to resent the boss's authority and to rebel against the boss's decisions. Sometimes a person will escalate a conflict beyond what is appropriate. Seeing the boss almost as an institutional enemy, this type of manager will often, without being conscious of it, fight with the boss just for the sake of fighting. The subordinate's reactions to being constrained are usually strong and sometimes impulsive. He or she sees the boss as someone who, by virtue of the role, is a hindrance to progress, an obstacle to be circumvented or at best tolerated.

Psychologists call this pattern of reactions counterdependent behavior. Although a counterdependent person is difficult for most superiors to manage and usually has a history of strained relationships with superiors, this sort of manager is apt to have even more trouble with a boss who tends to be directive or authoritarian. When the manager acts on his or her negative feelings, often in subtle and nonverbal ways, the boss sometimes does become the enemy. Sensing the subordinate's latent hostility, the boss will lose trust in the subordinate or his or her judgment and then behave even less openly.

Paradoxically, a manager with this type of predisposition is often a good manager of his or her own people. He or she will many times go out of the way to get support for them and will not hesitate to go to bat for them.

At the other extreme are managers who swallow their anger and behave in a very compliant fashion when the boss makes what they know to be a poor decision. These managers will agree with the boss even when a disagreement might be welcome or when the boss would easily alter a decision if given more information. Because they bear no relationship to the specific situation at hand, their responses are as much an overreaction as those of counterdependent managers. Instead of seeing the boss as an enemy, these people deny their anger—the other extreme—and tend to see the boss as if he or she were an all-wise parent who should know best, should take responsibility for their careers, train them in all they need to know, and protect them from overly ambitious peers.

Both counterdependence and overdependence lead managers to hold unrealistic views of what a boss is. Both views ignore that most bosses, like everyone else, are imperfect and fallible. They don't have unlimited time, encyclopedic knowledge, or extrasensory perception; nor are they evil enemies. They have their own pressures and concerns that are sometimes at odds with the wishes of the subordinate—and often for good reason.

Altering predispositions toward authority, especially at the extremes, is almost impossible without intensive psychotherapy (psychoanalytic theory and research suggest that such predispositions are deeply rooted in a person's personality and upbringing). However, an awareness of these extremes and the range between them can be very useful in understanding where your own predispositions fall and what the implications are for how you tend to behave in relation to your boss.

If you believe, on the one hand, that you have some tendencies toward counterdependence, you can understand and even predict what your reactions and overreactions are likely to be. If, on the other hand, you believe you have some tendencies toward overdependence, you might question the extent to which your overcompliance or inability to confront real differences may be making both you and your boss less effective.

Developing and Managing the Relationship

With a clear understanding of both your boss and yourself, you can *usually* establish a way of working together that fits both of you, that is characterized by unambiguous mutual expectations, and that helps you both be more productive and effective. The "Checklist for Managing Your Boss" (at the end of this article) summarizes some things such a relationship consists of. Following are a few more.

COMPATIBLE WORK STYLES

Above all else, a good working relationship with a boss accommodates differences in work style. For example, in one situation we studied, a manager (who had a relatively good relationship with his superior) realized that during meetings his boss would often become inattentive and sometimes brusque. The subordinate's own style tended to be discursive and exploratory. He would often digress from the topic at hand to deal with background factors, alternative approaches, and so forth. His boss preferred to discuss problems with a minimum of background detail and became impatient and distracted whenever his subordinate digressed from the immediate issue.

Recognizing this difference in style, the manager became terser and more direct during meetings with his boss. To help himself do this, before meetings, he would develop brief agendas that he used as a guide. Whenever he felt that a digression was needed, he explained why. This small shift in his own style made these meetings more effective and far less frustrating for both of them.

Subordinates can adjust their styles in response to their bosses' preferred method for receiving information. Peter Drucker divides bosses into "listeners" and "readers." Some bosses like to get information in report form so they can read and study it. Others work better with information and reports presented in person so they can ask questions. As Drucker points out, the implications are obvious. If your boss is a listener, you brief him or her in person, *then* follow it up with a memo. If your boss is a reader, you cover important items or proposals in a memo or report, *then* discuss them.

Other adjustments can be made according to a boss's decision-making style. Some bosses prefer to be involved in decisions and problems as they arise. These are high-involvement managers who like to keep their hands on the pulse of the operation. Usually their needs (and your own) are best satisfied if you touch base with them on an ad hoc basis. A boss who has a need to be involved will become involved one way or another, so there are advantages to including him or her at your initiative. Other bosses prefer to delegate—they don't want to be involved. They expect you to come to them with major problems and inform them about any important changes.

Creating a compatible relationship also involved drawing on each other's strengths and making up for each other's weaknesses. Because he knew that the boss—the vice president of engineering—was not very good at monitoring his employees' problems, one manager we studied made a point of doing it himself. The stakes were high: the engineers and technicians were all union members, the company worked on a customer-contract basis, and the company had recently experienced a serious strike.

The manager worked closely with his boss, along with people in the scheduling department and the personnel office, to make sure that potential problems were avoided. He also developed an informal arrangement through which his boss would review with him any proposed changes in personnel or assignment policies before taking action. The boss valued his advice and credited his subordinate for improving both the performance of the division and the labor-management climate.

MUTUAL EXPECTATIONS

The subordinate who passively assumes that he or she knows what the boss expects is in for trouble. Of course, some superiors will spell out their expectations very explicitly and in great detail. But most do not. And although many corporations have systems that provide a basis for communicating expectations (such as formal planning processes, career planning reviews, and performance appraisal reviews), these systems never work perfectly. Also, between these formal reviews, expectations invariably change.

Ultimately, the burden falls on the subordinate to find out what the boss's expectations are. They can be both broad (such as what kinds of problems the boss wishes to be informed about and when) as well as very specific (such things as when a particular project should be completed and what kinds of information the boss needs in the interim).

Getting a boss who tends to be vague or not explicit to express expectations can be difficult. But effective managers find ways to get that information. Some will draft a detailed memo covering key aspects of their work and then send it to their boss for approval. They then follow this up with a face-to-face discussion in which they go over each item in the memo. A discussion like this will often surface virtually all of the boss's expectations.

Other effective managers will deal with an inexplicit boss by initiating an ongoing series of informal discussions about "good management" and "our objectives." Still others find useful information more indirectly through those who used to work for the boss and through the formal planning systems in which the boss makes commitments to his or her own superior. Which approach you choose, of course, should depend on your understanding of your boss's style.

Developing a workable set of mutual expectations also requires that you communicate your own expectations to the boss, find out if they are realistic, and influence the boss to accept the ones that are important to you. Being able to influence the boss to value your expectations can be particularly important if the boss is an overachiever. Such a boss will often set unrealistically high standards that need to be brought into line with reality.

A FLOW OF INFORMATION

How much information a boss needs about what a subordinate is doing will vary significantly depending on the boss's style, the situation he or she is in, and the confidence the boss has in the subordinate. But it is not uncommon for a boss to need more information than the subordinate would naturally supply or for the subordinate to think the boss knows more than he or she really does. Effective managers recognize that they probably underestimate what their bosses need to know and make sure they find ways to keep them informed through processes that fit their styles.

Managing the flow of information upward is particularly difficult if the boss does not like to hear about problems. Although many people would deny it, bosses often give off signals they want to hear only good news. They show great displeasure—usually nonverbally—when someone tells them about a problem. Ignoring individual achievement, they may even evaluate more favorably subordinates who do not bring problems to them.

Nevertheless, for the good of the organization, the boss, and the subordinate, a superior needs to hear about failures as well as successes. Some subordinates deal with a good-news-only boss by finding indirect ways to get the necessary information to him or her, such as a management information system. Others see to it that potential problems, whether in the form of good surprises or bad news, are communicated immediately.

DEPENDABILITY AND HONESTY

Few things are more disabling to a boss than a subordinate on whom he cannot depend, whose work he cannot trust. Almost no one is intentionally undependable, but many managers are inadvertently so because of oversight or uncertainty about the boss's priorities. A commitment to an optimistic delivery date may please a superior in the short term but become a source of displeasure if not honored. It's difficult for a boss to rely on a subordinate who repeatedly slips deadlines. As one president (describing a subordinate) put it: "I'd rather he be more consistent even if he delivered fewer peak successes—at least I could rely on him."

Nor are many managers intentionally dishonest with their bosses. But it is easy to shade the truth and play down issues. Current concerns often become future surprise problems. It's almost impossible for bosses to work effectively if they cannot rely on a fairly accurate reading from their subordinates. Because it undermines credibility, dishonesty is perhaps the most troubling trait a subordinate can have. Without a basic level of trust, a boss feels compelled to check all of a subordinate's decisions, which makes it difficult to delegate.

GOOD USE OF TIME AND RESOURCES

Your boss is probably as limited in his or her store of time, energy, and influence as you are. Every request you make of your boss uses up some of these resources, so it's wise to draw on these resources selectively. This may sound obvious, but many managers use up their boss's time (and some of their own credibility) over relatively trivial issues.

One vice president went to great lengths to get his boss to fire a meddlesome secretary in another department. His boss had to use considerable influence to do it. Understandably, the head of the other department was not pleased. Later, when the vice president wanted to tackle more important problems, he ran into trouble. By using up blue chips on a relatively trivial issue, he had made it difficult for him and his boss to meet more important goals.

No doubt, some subordinates will resent that on top of all their other duties, they also need to take time and energy to manage their relationships with their bosses. Such managers fail to realize the importance of this activity and how it can simplify their jobs by eliminating potentially severe problems. Effective managers recognize that this part of their work is legitimate. Seeing themselves as ultimately responsible for what they achieve in an organization, they know they need to establish and manage relationships with everyone on whom they depend—and that includes the boss.

Checklist for Managing Your Boss

MAKE SURE YOU UNDERSTAND your boss and his or her context, including:

- Goals and objectives
- Pressures
- Strengths, weaknesses, blind spots
- Preferred work style

Assess yourself and your needs, including:

- Strengths and weaknesses
- Personal style
- Predisposition toward dependence on authority figures

Develop and maintain a relationship that:

- Fits both your needs and styles
- Is characterized by mutual expectations
- Keeps your boss informed
- Is based on dependability and honesty
- Selectively uses your boss's time and resources

Retrospective Commentary

"WHEN WE FIRST WROTE THIS ARTICLE late in 1979, the idea of managing your boss was an illegitimate notion," recalls John Gabarro. "Except for one article that Peter Drucker had written about 20 years earlier, there was nothing in management literature on the idea." At the time, Gabarro and coauthor John Kotter were working together on organizational behavior in the MBA course at Harvard Business School. Doing very different kinds of field research on effective managers, both found that managing one's own boss is crucial to success. So they immediately added a section on it to their course.

John Kotter had been concentrating on what a general manager's job is and how to do it effectively. He was finding that good general managers not only managed downward but also were effective in lateral relationships with peers and in working with their superiors. John Gabarro had found that effective managers handled lateral, upward, and downward relationships equally well. He developed four intensive case studies on how a new manager takes charge, later confirmed by 17 cases in his successful 1987 book, *The Dynamics of Taking Charge* (HBS Press).

The two young faculty members first combined their notes on managing your boss to teach students in their MBA course. At first, the students did not know what to make of it, John Gabarro reports. He was running up against the standard cynicism, as old as master-slave relationships, about apple polishing. In shop talk, the most savage jokes were reserved for those who nuzzle upward. Boss flattering and pampering seemed to dishonor both parties. If the boss is a wise, all-knowing figure of perfection, he or she does not need to be managed, people thought, who viewed such behavior as manipulation.

As Gabarro and Kotter developed more data, the value of boss managing became more and more clear to them. Their focus on what works—what behavior is effective—led them to an insight that still cuts through the folklore. Forget ambition. Forget promotion. Forget raises. Just think of the job and how to be effective in it. How do you get the resources you need—the information, the advice, even the permission to keep at it? The answers always point toward whoever has the power, the leverage—that is, the boss. To fail to make that relationship one of mutual respect and understanding is to miss a major factor in being effective.

As their thinking developed, Gabarro and Kotter realized they were on to something basic. They took their notes to an HBR editor, and she agreed right away to work with them on this landmark article. Published 13 years ago, in January-February 1990, "Managing Your Boss" is one of HBR's best-selling reprints. Now it takes its place as an HBR Classic, in that special category reserved for the all-time best.

Gabarro and Kotter continue their work together today at HBS, where last year they founded the Managerial Behavior Interest Group. Looking back on "Managing Your Boss," Kotter has one caution: "If we were writing the article today," he says, "I would worry a bit about managers who pay too much attention to managing upward."

—The Editors

Originally published in May–June 1993
Reprint 93306

A Survival Guide for Leaders

RONALD A. HEIFETZ AND MARTY LINSKY

Executive Summary

LET'S FACE IT, to lead is to live dangerously. While leadership is often viewed as an exciting and glamorous endeavor, one in which you inspire others to follow you through good times and bad, such a portrayal ignores leadership's dark side: the inevitable attempts to take you out of the game.

This is particularly true when a leader must steer an organization through difficult change. When the status quo is upset, people feel a sense of profound loss and dashed expectations. They may need to undergo a period of feeling incompetent or disloyal. It's no wonder they resist the change and often try to eliminate its visible agent.

This "survival guide" offers a number of techniques— relatively straightforward in concept but difficult to execute—for protecting yourself as you lead such a change initiative. Adapted from the book *Leadership on the Line: Staying Alive Through the Dangers of Leading* (Harvard Business School Press, 2002), the article has two main parts. The first looks outward, offering tactical advice about relating to your organization and the people in it. It is designed to protect you from those who would push you aside before you complete your initiatives. The second looks inward, focusing on your own needs and vulnerabilities. It is designed to keep you from bringing yourself down.

The hard truth is that it is not possible to experience the rewards and joys of leadership without experiencing the pain as well. But staying in the game and bearing that pain is worth it, not only for the positive changes you can make in the lives of others but also for the meaning it gives your own.

T HINK OF THE MANY top executives in recent years who, sometimes after long periods of considerable success, have crashed and burned. Or think of individuals you have known in less prominent positions, perhaps people spearheading significant change initiatives in their organizations, who have suddenly found themselves out of a job. Think about yourself: In exercising leadership, have *you* ever been removed or pushed aside?

Let's face it, to lead is to live dangerously. While leadership is often depicted as an exciting and glamorous endeavor, one in which you inspire others to follow you through good times and bad, such a portrayal ignores leadership's dark side: the inevitable attempts to take you out of the game.

Those attempts are sometimes justified. People in top positions must often pay the price for a flawed strategy or a series of bad decisions. But frequently, something more is at work. We're not talking here about conventional office politics; we're talking about the high-stake risks you face whenever you try to lead an organization through difficult but necessary change. The risks during such times are especially high because change that truly transforms an organization, be it a multibillion-dollar company or a ten-person sales team, demands that people give up things they hold dear: daily habits, loyalties, ways of thinking. In return for these sacrifices, they may be offered nothing more than the possibility of a better future.

We refer to this kind of wrenching organizational transformation as "adaptive change," something very different from the "technical change" that occupies people in positions of authority on a regular basis. Technical problems, while often challenging, can be solved applying existing know-how and the organization's current problem-solving processes. Adaptive problems resist these kinds of solutions because they require individuals throughout the organization to alter their ways; as the people themselves are the problem, the solution lies with them. (See "Adaptive Versus Technical Change: Whose Problem Is It?" at the end of this article.) Responding to an adaptive challenge with a technical fix may have some short-term appeal. But to make real progress, sooner or later those who lead must ask themselves and the people in the organization to face a set of deeper issues—and to accept a solution that may require turning part or all of the organization upside down.

It is at this point that danger lurks. And most people who lead in such a situation—swept up in the action, championing a cause they believe in—are caught unawares. Over and over again, we have seen courageous souls blissfully ignorant of an approaching threat until it was too late to respond.

The hazard can take numerous forms. You may be attacked directly in an attempt to shift the debate to your character and style and avoid discussion of your initiative. You may be marginalized, forced into the position of becoming so identified with one issue that your broad authority is undermined. You may be seduced by your supporters and, fearful of losing their approval and affection, fail to demand they make the sacrifices needed for the initiative to succeed. You may be diverted from your goal by people overwhelming you with the day-to-day details of carrying it out, keeping you busy and pre-occupied.

Each one of these thwarting tactics—whether done consciously or not—grows out of people's aversion to the organizational disequilibrium created by your initiative. By attempting to undercut you, people strive to restore order, maintain what is familiar to them, and protect themselves from the pains of adaptive change. They want to be comfortable again, and you're in the way.

So how do you protect yourself? Over a combined 50 years of teaching and consulting, we have asked ourselves that question time and again—usually while watching top-notch and well-intentioned folks get taken out of the game. On occasion, the question has become painfully personal; we as individuals have been knocked off course or out of the action more than once in our own leadership efforts. So we are offering what we hope are some pragmatic answers that grow out of these observations and experiences. We should note that while our advice clearly applies to senior executives, it also applies to people trying to lead change initiatives from positions of little or no formal organizational authority.

This "survival guide" has two main parts. The first looks outward, offering tactical advice about relating to your organization and the people in it. It is designed to protect you from those trying to push you aside before you complete your initiative. The second looks inward, focusing on your own human needs and vulnerabilities. It is designed to keep you from bringing yourself down.

A Hostile Environment

Leading major organizational change often involves radically reconfiguring a complex network of people, tasks, and institutions that have achieved a kind of modus vivendi, no matter how dysfunctional it appears to you. When the status quo is upset, people feel a sense of profound loss and dashed expectations. They may go through a period of feeling incompetent or disloyal. It's no wonder they resist the change or try to eliminate its visible agent. We offer here a number of techniques—relatively straightforward in concept but difficult to execute—for minimizing these external threats.

OPERATE IN AND ABOVE THE FRAY

The ability to maintain perspective in the midst of action is critical to lowering resistance. Any military officer knows the importance of maintaining the capacity for reflection, especially in the "fog of war." Great athletes must simultaneously play the game and observe it as a whole. We call this skill "getting off the dance floor and going to the balcony," an image that captures the mental activity of stepping back from the action and asking, "What's really going on here?"

Leadership is an improvisational art. You may be guided by an overarching vision, clear values, and a strategic plan, but what you actually do from moment to moment cannot be scripted. You must respond as events unfold. To use our metaphor, you have to move back and forth from the balcony to the dance floor, over and over again throughout the days, weeks, months, and years. While today's plan may make sense now, tomorrow you'll discover the unanticipated effects of today's actions and have to adjust accordingly. Sustaining good leadership, then, requires first and foremost the capacity to see what is happening to you and your initiative as it is happening and to understand how today's turns in the road will affect tomorrow's plans.

But taking a balcony perspective is extremely tough to do when you're fiercely engaged down below, being pushed and pulled by the events and people around you—and doing some pushing and pulling of your own. Even if you are able to break away, the practice of stepping back and seeing the big picture is complicated by several factors. For example, when you get some distance, you still must accurately interpret what you see and hear. This is easier said than done. In an attempt to avoid difficult change, people will naturally, even unconsciously, defend their habits and ways of thinking. As you seek input from a broad range of people, you'll constantly need to be aware of these hidden agendas. You'll also need to observe your own actions; seeing yourself

Executives leading difficult change initiatives are often blissfully ignorant of an approaching threat until it is too late to respond.

objectively as you look down from the balcony is perhaps the hardest task of all.

Fortunately, you can learn to be both an observer and a participant at the same time. When you are sitting in a meeting, practice by watching what is happening while it is happening—even as you are part of what is happening. Observe the relationships and see how people's attention to one another can vary: supporting, thwarting, or listening. Watch people's body language. When you make a point, resist the instinct to stay perched on the edge of your seat, ready to defend what you said. A technique as simple as pushing your chair a few inches away from the table after you speak may provide the literal as well as metaphorical distance you need to become an observer.

COURT THE UNCOMMITTED

It's tempting to go it alone when leading a change initiative. There's no one to dilute your ideas or share the glory, and it's often just plain exciting. It's also foolish. You need to recruit partners, people who can help protect you from attacks and who can point out potentially fatal flaws in your strategy or initiative. Moreover, you are far less vulnerable when you are out on the point with a bunch of folks rather than alone. You also need to keep the opposition close. Knowing what your opponents are thinking can help you challenge them more effectively and thwart their attempts to upset your agenda—or allow you to borrow ideas that will improve your initiative. Have coffee once a week with the person most dedicated to seeing you fail.

But while relationships with allies and opponents are essential, the people who will determine your success are often those in the middle, the uncommitted who nonetheless are wary of your plans. They have no substantive stake in your initiative, but they do have a stake in the comfort, stability, and security of the status quo. They've seen change agents come and go, and they know that your initiative will disrupt their lives and make their futures uncertain. You want to be sure that this general uneasiness doesn't evolve into a move to push you aside.

These people will need to see that your intentions are serious—for example, that you are willing to let go of those who can't make the changes your initiative requires. But people must also see that you understand the loss you are asking them to accept. You need to name the loss, be it a change in time-honored work routines or an overhaul of the company's core values, and explicitly acknowledge the resulting pain. You might do this through a series of simple statements, but it often requires something more tangible and public—recall Franklin Roosevelt's radio "fireside chats" during the Great Depression—to convince people that you truly understand.

Beyond a willingness to accept casualties and acknowledge people's losses, two very personal types of action can defuse potential resistance to you and your initiatives. The first is practicing what you preach. In 1972, Gene Patterson took over as editor of the *St. Petersburg Times*. His mandate was to take the respected regional newspaper to a higher level, enhancing its reputation for fine writing while becoming a fearless and hard-hitting news source. This would require major changes not only in the way the community viewed the newspaper but also in the way *Times* reporters thought about themselves and their roles. Because prominent organizations and individuals would no longer be spared warranted criticism, reporters would sometimes be angrily rebuked by the subjects of articles.

Several years after Patterson arrived, he attended a party at the home of the paper's foreign editor. Driving home, he pulled up to a red light and scraped the car next to him. The police officer called to the scene charged Patterson with driving under the influence. Patterson phoned Bob Haiman, a veteran *Times* newsman who had just been appointed executive editor, and insisted that a story on his arrest be run. As Haiman recalls, he tried to talk Patterson out of it, arguing that DUI arrests that didn't involve injuries were rarely reported, even when prominent figures were involved. Patterson was adamant, however, and insisted that the story appear on page one.

To neutralize potential opposition, you should acknowledge your own responsibility for whatever problems the organization currently faces.

Patterson, still viewed as somewhat of an outsider at the paper, knew that if he wanted his employees to follow the highest journalistic standards, he would have to display those standards, even when it hurt. Few leaders are called upon to disgrace themselves on the front page of a newspaper. But adopting the behavior you expect from others—whether it be taking a pay cut in tough times or spending a day working next to employees on a reconfigured production line—can be crucial in getting buy-in from people who might try to undermine your initiative.

The second thing you can do to neutralize potential opposition is to acknowledge your own responsibility for whatever problems the organization currently faces. If you have been with the company for some time, whether in a position of senior authority or not, you've likely contributed in some way to the current mess. Even if you are new, you need to identify areas of your own behavior that could stifle the change you hope to make.

In our teaching, training, and consulting, we often ask people to write or talk about a leadership challenge they currently face. Over the years, we have read and heard literally thousands of such challenges. Typically, in the first version of the story, the author is nowhere to be found. The underlying message: "If only other people would shape up, I could make progress here." But by too readily pointing your finger at others, you risk making yourself a target. Remember, you are asking people to move to a place where they are frightened to go. If at the same time you're blaming them for having to go there, they will undoubtedly turn against you.

In the early 1990s, Leslie Wexner, founder and CEO of the Limited, realized the need for major changes at the company, including a significant reduction in the workforce. But his consultant told him that something else had to change: long-standing habits that were at the heart of his self-image. In particular, he had to stop treating the company as if it were his family. The indulgent father had to become the chief personnel officer, putting the right people in the right jobs and holding them accountable for their work. "I was an athlete trained to be a baseball player," Wexner recalled during a recent speech at Harvard's Kennedy School. "And one day, someone tapped me on the shoulder and said, 'Football.' And I said, 'No, I'm a baseball player.' And he said, 'Football.' And I said, 'I don't know how to play football. I'm not 6'4", and I don't weigh 300 pounds.' But if no one values baseball anymore, the baseball player will be out of business. So I looked into the mirror and said, 'Schlemiel, nobody wants to watch baseball. Make the transformation to football.'" His personal makeover—shedding the role of forgiving father to those widely viewed as not holding their own—helped sway other employees to back a corporate makeover. And his willingness to change helped protect him from attack during the company's long—and generally successful—turnaround period.

COOK THE CONFLICT

Managing conflict is one of the greatest challenges a leader of organizational change faces. The conflict may involve resistance to change, or it may involve clashing viewpoints about how the change should be carried out. Often, it will be latent rather than palpable. That's because most organizations are allergic to conflict, seeing it primarily as a source of danger, which it certainly can be. But conflict is a necessary part of the change process and, if handled properly, can serve as the engine of progress.

Thus, a key imperative for a leader trying to achieve significant change is to manage people's passionate differences in a way that diminishes their destructive potential and constructively harnesses their energy. Two techniques can help you achieve this. First, create a secure place where the conflicts can freely bubble up. Second, control the temperature to ensure that the conflict doesn't boil over—and burn you in the process.

The vessel in which a conflict is simmered—in which clashing points of view mix, lose some of their sharpness, and ideally blend into consensus—will look and feel quite different in different contexts. It may be a protected physical space, perhaps an off-site location where an outside facilitator helps a group work through its differences. It may be a clear set of rules and processes that give minority voices confidence that they will be heard without having to disrupt the proceedings to gain attention. It may be the shared language and history of an organization that binds people together through trying times. Whatever its form, it is a place or a means to contain the roiling forces unleashed by the threat of major change.

But a vessel can withstand only so much strain before it blows. A huge challenge you face as a leader is keeping your employees' stress at a productive level. The success of the change effort—as well as your own authority and even survival—requires you to monitor your organization's tolerance for heat and then regulate the temperature accordingly.

You first need to raise the heat enough that people sit up, pay attention, and deal with the real threats and challenges facing them. After all, without some distress, there's no incentive to change. You can constructively raise the temperature by focusing people's attention on the hard issues, by forcing them to take responsibility for tackling and solving those issues, and by bringing conflicts occurring behind closed doors out into the open.

But you have to lower the temperature when necessary to reduce what can be counterproductive turmoil. You can turn down the heat by slowing the pace of change or by tackling some relatively straightforward technical aspect of the problem, thereby reducing people's anxiety levels and allowing them to get warmed up for bigger challenges. You can provide structure to the problem-solving process, creating work groups with specific assignments, setting time parameters, establishing rules for decision making, and outlining reporting relationships. You can use humor or find an excuse for a break or a party to temporarily ease tensions. You can speak to people's fears and, more critically, to their hopes for a more promising future. By showing people how the future might look, you come to embody hope rather than fear, and you reduce the likelihood of becoming a lightning rod for the conflict.

The aim of both these tactics is to keep the heat high enough to motivate people but low enough to prevent a disastrous explosion—what we call a "productive range of distress." Remember, though, that most employees will reflexively want you to turn down the heat; their complaints may in fact indicate that the environment is just right for hard work to get done.

We've already mentioned a classic example of managing the distress of fundamental change: Franklin Roosevelt during the first few years of his presidency. When he took office in 1933, the chaos, tension, and anxiety brought on by the Depression ran extremely high. Demagogues stoked class, ethnic, and racial conflict that threatened to tear the nation apart. Individuals feared an uncertain future. So Roosevelt first did what he could to reduce the sense of disorder to a tolerable level. He took decisive and authoritative action—he pushed an extraordinary number of bills through Congress during his fabled first 100 days—and thereby gave Americans a sense of direction and safety, reassuring them that they were in capable hands. In his fireside chats, he spoke to people's anxiety and anger and laid out a positive vision for the future that made the stress of the current crisis bearable and seem a worthwhile price to pay for progress.

But he knew the problems facing the nation couldn't be solved from the White House. He needed to mobilize citizens and get them to dream up, try out, fight over, and ultimately own the sometimes painful solutions that would transform the country and move it forward. To do that, he needed to maintain a certain level of fermentation and distress. So, for example, he orchestrated conflicts over public priorities and programs among the large cast of creative people he brought into the government. By giving the same assignment to two different administrators and refusing to clearly define their roles, he got them to generate new and competing ideas. Roosevelt displayed both the acuity to recognize when the tension in the nation had risen too high and the emotional strength to take the heat and permit considerable anxiety to persist.

PLACE THE WORK WHERE IT BELONGS

Because major change requires people across an entire organization to adapt, you as a leader need to resist the reflex reaction of providing people with the answers. Instead, force yourself to transfer, as Roosevelt did, much of the work and problem solving to others. If you don't, real and sustainable change won't occur. In addition, it's risky on a personal level to continue to hold on to the work that should be done by others.

As a successful executive, you have gained credibility and authority by demonstrating your capacity to solve other people's problems. This ability can be a virtue, until you find yourself faced with a situation in which you cannot deliver solutions. When this happens, all of your habits, pride, and sense of competence get thrown out of kilter because you must mobilize the work of others rather than find the way yourself. By trying to solve an adaptive challenge for people, at best you will reconfigure it as a technical problem and create some short-term relief. But the issue will not have gone away.

In the 1994 National Basketball Association Eastern Conference semifinals, the Chicago Bulls lost to the New York Knicks in the first two games of the best-of-seven series. Chicago was out to prove that it was more than just a one-man team, that it could win without Michael Jordan, who had retired at the end of the previous season.

In the third game, the score was tied at 102 with less than two seconds left. Chicago had the ball and a time-out to plan a final shot. Coach Phil Jackson called for Scottie Pippen, the Bulls' star since Jordan had retired, to make the inbound pass to Toni Kukoc for the final shot. As play was about to resume, Jackson noticed Pippen sitting at the far end of the bench. Jackson asked him whether he was in or out. "I'm out," said Pippen, miffed that he was not tapped to take the final shot. With only four players on the floor, Jackson quickly called another time-out and substituted an excellent passer, the reserve Pete Myers, for Pippen. Myers tossed a perfect pass to Kukoc, who spun around and sank a miraculous shot to win the game.

The Bulls made their way back to the locker room, their euphoria deflated by Pippen's extraordinary act of insubordination. Jackson recalls that as he entered a silent room, he was uncertain about what to do. Should he punish Pippen? Make him apologize? Pretend the whole thing never happened? All eyes were on him. The coach looked around, meeting the gaze of each player, and said, "What happened has hurt us. Now you have to work this out."

Jackson knew that if he took action to resolve the immediate crisis, he would have made Pippen's behavior a matter between coach and player. But he understood that a deeper issue was at the heart of the incident: Who were the Chicago Bulls without Michael Jordan? It wasn't about who was going to succeed Jordan, because no one was; it was about whether the players could jell as a team where no one person dominated and every player was willing to do whatever it took to help. The issue rested with the players, not him, and only they could resolve it. It did not matter what they decided at that moment; what mattered was that they, not Jackson, did the deciding. What followed was a discussion led by an emotional Bill Cartwright, a team veteran. According to Jackson, the conversation brought the team closer together. The Bulls took the series to a seventh game before succumbing to the Knicks.

Jackson gave the work of addressing both the Pippen and the Jordan issues back to the team for another reason: If he had taken ownership of the problem, he would have become the issue, at least for the moment. In his case, his position as coach probably wouldn't have been threatened. But in other situations, taking responsibility for resolving a conflict within the organization poses risks. You are likely to find yourself resented by the faction that you decide against and held responsible by nearly everyone for the turmoil your decision generates. In the eyes of many, the only way to neutralize the threat is to get rid of you.

Despite that risk, most executives can't resist the temptation to solve fundamental organizational problems by themselves. People expect you to get right in there and fix things, to take a stand and resolve the problem. After all, that is what top managers are paid to do. When you fulfill those expectations, people will call you admirable and courageous—even a "leader"—and that is flattering. But challenging your employees' expectations requires greater courage and leadership.

The Dangers Within

We have described a handful of leadership tactics you can use to interact with the people around you, particularly those who might undermine your initiatives. Those tactics can help advance your initiatives and, just as important, ensure that you remain in a position where you can bring them to fruition. But from our own observations and painful personal experiences, we know that one of the surest ways for an organization to bring you down is simply to let you precipitate your own demise.

In the heat of leadership, with the adrenaline pumping, it is easy to convince yourself that you are not subject to the normal human frailties that can defeat ordinary mortals. You begin to act as if you are indestructible. But the intellectual, physical, and emotional challenges of leadership are fierce. So, in addition to getting on the balcony, you need to regularly step into the inner chamber of your being and assess the tolls those challenges are taking. If you don't, your seemingly indestructible self can self-destruct. This, by the way, is an ideal outcome for your foes—and even friends who oppose your initiative—because no one has to feel responsible for your downfall.

MANAGE YOUR HUNGERS

We all have hungers, expressions of our normal human needs. But sometimes those hungers disrupt our capacity to act wisely or purposefully. Whether inherited or products of our upbringing, some of these hungers may be so strong that they render us constantly vulnerable. More typically, a stressful situation or setting can exaggerate a normal level of need, amplifying our desires and overwhelming our usual self-discipline. Two of the most common and dangerous hungers are the desire for control and the desire for importance.

Everyone wants to have some measure of control over his or her life. Yet some people's need for control is disproportionately high. They might have grown up in a household that was either tightly structured or unusually chaotic; in either case, the situation drove them to become masters at taming chaos not only in their own lives but also in their organizations.

That need for control can be a source of vulnerability. Initially, of course, the ability to turn disorder into order may be seen as an attribute. In an organization facing turmoil, you may seem like a godsend if you are able (and desperately want) to step in and take charge. By lowering the distress to a tolerable level, you keep the kettle from boiling over.

But in your desire for order, you can mistake the means for the end. Rather than ensuring that the distress level in an organization remains high enough to mobilize progress on the issues, you focus on maintaining order as an end in itself. Forcing people to make the difficult trade-offs required by fundamental change threatens a return to the disorder you loathe. Your ability to bring the situation under control also suits the people in the organization, who naturally prefer calm to chaos. Unfortunately, this desire for control makes you vulnerable to, and an agent of, the organization's wish to avoid working through contentious issues. While this may ensure your survival in the short term, ultimately you may find yourself accused, justifiably, of failing to deal with the tough challenges when there was still time to do so.

Most people also have some need to feel important and affirmed by others. The danger here is that you will let this affirmation give you an inflated view of yourself and your cause. A grandiose sense of self-importance often leads to self-deception. In particular, you tend to forget the creative role that doubt—which reveals parts of reality that you wouldn't otherwise see—plays in getting your organization to improve. The absence of doubt leads you to see only that which confirms your own competence, which will virtually guarantee disastrous missteps.

Another harmful side effect of an inflated sense of self-importance is that you will encourage people in the organization to become dependent on you. The higher the level of distress, the greater their hopes and expectations that you will provide deliverance. This relieves them of any responsibility for moving the organization forward. But their dependence can be detrimental not only to the group but to you personally. Dependence can quickly turn to contempt as your constituents discover your human shortcomings.

Two well-known stories from the computer industry illustrate the perils of dependency—and how to avoid them. Ken Olsen, the founder of Digital Equipment Corporation, built the company into a 120,000-person operation that, at its peak, was the chief rival of IBM. A generous man, he treated his employees extraordinarily well and experimented with personnel policies designed to increase the creativity, teamwork, and satisfaction of his workforce. This, in tandem with the company's success over the years, led the company's top management to

To survive, you need a sanctuary where you can reflect on the previous day's journey, renew your emotional resources, and recalibrate your moral compass.

turn to him as the sole decision maker on all key issues. His decision to shun the personal computer market because of his belief that few people would ever want to own a PC, which seemed reasonable at the time, is generally viewed as the beginning of the end for the company. But that isn't the point; everyone in business makes bad decisions. The point is, Olsen had fostered such an atmosphere of dependence that his decisions were rarely challenged by colleagues—at least not until it was too late.

Contrast that decision with Bill Gates's decision some years later to keep Microsoft out of the Internet business. It didn't take long for him to reverse his stand and launch a corporate overhaul that had Microsoft's delivery of Internet services as its centerpiece. After watching the rapidly changing computer industry and listening carefully to colleagues, Gates changed his mind with no permanent damage to his sense of pride and an enhanced reputation due to his nimble change of course.

ANCHOR YOURSELF

To survive the turbulent seas of a change initiative, you need to find ways to steady and stabilize yourself. First, you must establish a safe harbor where each day you can reflect on the previous day's journey, repair the psychological damage you have incurred, renew your stores of emotional resources, and recalibrate your moral compass. Your haven might be a physical place, such as the kitchen table of a friend's house, or a regular routine, such as a daily walk through the neighborhood. Whatever the sanctuary, you need to use and protect it. Unfortunately, seeking such respite is often seen as a luxury, making it one of the first things to go when life gets stressful and you become pressed for time.

Second, you need a confidant, someone you can talk to about what's in your heart and on your mind without fear of being judged or betrayed. Once the undigested mess is on the table, you can begin to separate, with your confidant's honest input, what is worthwhile from what is simply venting. The confidant, typically not a coworker, can also pump you up when you're down and pull you back to earth when you start taking praise too seriously. But don't confuse confidants with allies: Instead of supporting your current initiative, a confidant simply supports you. A common mistake is to seek a confidant among trusted allies, whose personal loyalty may evaporate when a new issue more important to them than you begins to emerge and take center stage.

Perhaps most important, you need to distinguish between your personal self, which can serve as an anchor in stormy weather, and your professional role, which never will. It is easy to mix up the two. And other people only increase the confusion: Colleagues, subordinates, and even bosses often act as if the role you play is the real you. But that is not the case, no matter how much of yourself—your passions, your values, your talents—you genuinely and laudably pour into your professional role. Ask anyone who has experienced the rude awakening that comes when they leave a position of authority and suddenly find that their phone calls aren't returned as quickly as they used to be.

That harsh lesson holds another important truth that is easily forgotten: When people attack someone in a position of authority, more often than not they are attacking the role, not the person. Even when attacks on you are highly personal, you need to read them primarily as reactions to how you, in your role, are affecting people's lives. Understanding the criticism for what it is prevents it from undermining your stability and sense of self-worth. And that's important because when you feel the sting of an attack, you are likely to become defensive and lash out at your critics, which can precipitate your downfall.

We hasten to add that criticism may contain legitimate points about how you are performing your role. For example, you may have been tactless in raising an issue with your organization, or you may have turned the heat up too quickly on a change initiative. But, at its heart, the criticism is usually about the issue, not you. Through the guise of attacking you personally, people often are simply trying to neutralize the threat they perceive in your point of view. Does anyone ever attack you when you hand out big checks or deliver good news? People attack your personality, style, or judgment when they don't like the message.

When you take "personal" attacks personally, you unwittingly conspire in one of the common ways you can be taken out of action—you make yourself the issue. Contrast the manner in which presidential candidates Gary Hart and Bill Clinton handled charges of philandering. Hart angrily counterattacked, criticizing the scruples of the reporters who had shadowed him. This defensive personal response kept the focus on his behavior. Clinton, on national television, essentially admitted he had strayed, acknowledging his piece of the mess. His strategic handling of the situation allowed him to return the campaign's focus to policy issues. Though both attacks were extremely personal, only Clinton understood that they were basically attacks on positions he represented and the role he was seeking to play.

Do not underestimate the difficulty of distinguishing self from role and responding coolly to what feels like a personal attack—particularly when the criticism comes, as it will, from people you care about. But disciplining yourself to do so can provide you with an anchor that will keep you from running aground and give you the stability to remain calm, focused, and persistent in engaging people with the tough issues.

Why Lead?

We will have failed if this "survival manual" for avoiding the perils of leadership causes you to become cynical or callous in your leadership effort or to shun the challenges of leadership altogether. We haven't touched on the thrill of inspiring people to come up with creative solutions that can transform an organization for the better. We hope we have shown that the essence of leadership lies in the capacity to deliver disturbing news and raise difficult questions in a way that moves people to take up the message rather than kill the messenger. But we haven't talked about the reasons that someone might want to take these risks.

Of course, many people who strive for high-authority positions are attracted to power. But in the end, that isn't enough to make the high stakes of the game worthwhile. We would argue that, when they look deep within themselves, people grapple with the challenges of leadership in order to make a positive difference in the lives of others.

When corporate presidents and vice presidents reach their late fifties, they often look back on careers devoted to winning in the marketplace. They may have succeeded remarkably, yet some people have difficulty making sense of their lives in light of what they have given up. For too many, their accomplishments seem empty. They question whether they should have been more aggressive in questioning corporate purposes or creating more ambitious visions for their companies.

Our underlying assumption in this article is that you can lead *and* stay alive—not just register a pulse, but really be alive. But the classic protective devices of a person in authority tend to insulate them from those qualities that foster an acute experience of living. Cynicism, often dressed up as realism, undermines creativity and daring. Arrogance, often posing as authoritative knowledge, snuffs out curiosity and the eagerness to question. Callousness, sometimes portrayed as the thick skin of experience, shuts out compassion for others.

The hard truth is that it is not possible to know the rewards and joys of leadership without experiencing the pain as well. But staying in the game and bearing that pain is worth it, not only for the positive changes you can make in the lives of others but also for the meaning it gives your own.

Adaptive Versus Technical Change Whose Problem Is It?

THE IMPORTANCE—AND DIFFICULTY—of distinguishing between adaptive and technical change can be illustrated with an analogy. When your car has problems, you go to a mechanic. Most of the time, the mechanic can fix the car. But if your car troubles stem from the way a family member drives, the problems are likely to recur. Treating the problems as purely technical ones—taking the car to the mechanic time and again to get it back on the road—masks the real issues. Maybe you need to get your mother to stop drinking and driving, get your grand-father to give up his driver's license, or get your teenager to be more cautious. Whatever the underlying problems, the mechanic can't solve them. Instead, changes in the family need to occur, and that won't be easy. People will resist the moves, even denying that such problems exist. That's because even those not directly affected by an adaptive change typically experience discomfort when someone upsets a group's or an organization's equilibrium.

Such resistance to adaptive change certainly happens in business. Indeed, it's the classic error: Companies treat adaptive challenges as if they were technical problems. For example, executives attempt to improve the bottom line by cutting costs across the board. Not only does this avoid the need to make tough choices about which areas should be trimmed, it also masks the fact that the company's real challenge lies in redesigning its strategy.

Treating adaptive challenges as technical ones permits executives to do what they have excelled at throughout their careers: solve other people's problems. And it allows others in the organization to enjoy the primordial peace of mind that comes from knowing that their commanding officer has a plan to maintain order and stability. After all, the executive doesn't have to instigate—and the people don't have to undergo—uncomfortable change. Most people would agree that, despite the selective pain of a cost-cutting exercise, it is less traumatic than reinventing a company.

Originally published in June 2002
Reprint R0206C

About the Contributors

RICHARD BOYATZIS is Professor of Organizational Behavior and Chair of the Department of Organizational Behavior at the Weatherhead School of Management at Case Western Reserve University. He has written numerous articles and books on human motivation, leadership, managerial competencies, and the development of competencies and emotional intelligence. His latest book, with Daniel Goleman and Annie McKee, *Primal Leadership: Realizing the Power of Emotional Intelligence*, is an international best-seller.

VIVIEN CORWIN is a professor at Royal Roads University in British Columbia. She researches in the area of strategic human resource management, focusing primarily on changes in the employment relationship, specifically organizational culture, organizational commitment, and nontraditional working arrangements. Prior to attending UBC for her Ph.D., Vivien completed a B.A. degree in International Relations, with an English minor, at the University of Toronto.

PETER F. DRUCKER is a writer, teacher and consultant. He has published thirty-four books, which have been translated into more than thirty languages. Drucker has been the Clarke Professor of Social Science and Management at the Claremont Graduate University in Claremont, CA. He is a consultant specializing in strategy and policy for both businesses and nonprofits, and in the work and organization of top management. Born in 1909 in Vienna, Austria, Drucker was educated in Austria and in England. He holds a doctorate in Public and International Law from Frankfurt University (Germany). He is married and has four children and six grandchildren.

PETER J. FROST holds the Edgar F. Kaiser Chair in Organizational Behavior in the Faculty of Commerce and Business Administration at The University of British Columbia. For the past twenty-five years he has studied and written about issues of leadership, with particular attention to organizational culture and to emotions in the workplace. His work has been published in the top academic and professional journals in his field, and he is the author/editor of more than a dozen books on organizational issues and practices. His forthcoming book is *Toxic Emotions at Work* (Harvard Business School Press, 2003).

JOHN J. GABARRO is the UPS Foundation Professor of Human Resource Management and Faculty Chair of the Advanced Management Program at the Harvard Business School. Gabarro's research has focused on organizational change, managerial effectiveness, and executive succession. He is the author or co-author of six books, one of the most recent of which is *Breaking Through* with David A. Thomas, which won the 2001 George Terry Prize, given by the Academy of Management for outstanding contribution to management theory and practice. Gabarro completed his M.B.A., doctorate, and postdoctoral work at Harvard before joining the faculty.

DANIEL GOLEMAN is the author of the best-selling books *Emotional Intelligence* and *Working with Emotional Intelligence* and coauthor of *Primal Leadership: Realizing the Power*

of Emotional Intelligence with Annie McKee and Richard
Boyzatis. A trained psychologist, he worked for many years for
the *New York Times*, covering the brain and behavioral sci-
ences. He has also been a visiting faculty member at Harvard
University. Dr. Goleman is co-Chair of the Consortium for
Research on Emotional Intelligence in Organization at Rut-
gers University, and a founder of the Collaborative Social and
Emotional Learning at the University of Illinois at Chicago.
Through an affiliation with Hay Group he consults on leader-
ship and organization development worldwide.

RONALD A. HEIFETZ is Cofounder of the Center for Public
Leadership at Harvard University's John F. Kennedy School of
Government and a Principal of Cambridge Leadership Associates. His research at Harvard focuses on how to build adaptive capacity in societies, businesses, and nonprofits. His
widely acclaimed book, *Leadership Without Easy Answers* (the
Belknap Press of Harvard University Press, 1994), has been
translated into many languages and is currently in its twelfth
printing. His new book, *Leadership on the Line: Staying Alive
through the Dangers of Leading*, written with Marty Linsky,
was published in May 2002 by Harvard Business School Press.
A graduate of Columbia University, Harvard Medical School,
and the John F. Kennedy School of Government, Heifetz is
both a physician and a cellist, having studied with the Russian
virtuoso, Gregor Piatigorsky. Heifetz lives in the Boston area
with his wife, Sousan Abadian, and their two children.

RANDY KOMISAR partners with entrepreneurs creating
companies with leading-edge technologies, working with
executive teams to create business models, raise capital,
establish strategic relationships, and mentor senior management. He has founded companies such as Claris Corporation,
served as CEO for LucasArts Entertainment and Crystal
Dynamics, and acted as a "Virtual CEO" for such companies

as WebTV and MondoMedia. He currently sits on the board of TiVo and several privately held companies. Randy holds a B.A. in Economics from Brown University, is a graduate of the Harvard Law School, a Consulting Professor at Stanford University, and author of the best-selling book *The Monk and the Riddle*.

JOHN P. KOTTER is a graduate of MIT and Harvard. He is the author of six books that have won awards or honors and seven that have been business best-sellers. In October 2001, *BusinessWeek* magazine reported a survey they conducted of 504 enterprises that rated Professor Kotter the number-one "leadership guru" in America. He lives in Cambridge, Massachusetts, and in Ashland, New Hampshire, with wife Nancy Dearman, daughter Caroline, and son Jonathan.

THOMAS B. LAWRENCE is the Weyerhaeuser Professor of Change Management at Simon Fraser University in Vancouver, Canada. His research and teaching interests center on the role of power and institutions in the dynamics of organizational change. For the past ten years, he has been involved in a study of interorganizational collaboration that has examined these issues in a wide range of contexts, including nutrition services in the West Bank and Gaza, HIV/AIDS treatment in Canada, and the commercial whale-watching industry in British Columbia. Dr. Lawrence's research has been published in a variety of academic journals, including *Academy of Management Journal, Academy of Management Review, Journal of Management, Human Relations*, and *Journal of Management Studies*.

HARRY LEVINSON, PH.D., is Clinical Professor of Psychology Emeritus, Department of Psychiatry, Harvard Medical School; retired Chairman of the Levinson Institute; and former head of the section on Organizational Mental Health at the Massachusetts Mental Health Center. Dr. Levinson created and directed the Division of Industrial Mental Health of the Menninger Foundation. He is past president of the American Board of Professional Psychology. Dr. Levinson has authored numerous articles and sixteen books.

MARTY LINSKY has been on the faculty of the John F. Kennedy School of Government since 1982, except for 1992–1995 when he served as Chief Secretary and Counselor to Massachusetts Governor William Weld. He is Cofounder, with Dr. Ronald Heifetz, of Cambridge Leadership Associates, a leadership consulting, training, and coaching firm. He is a consultant, facilitator, and trainer in leadership, ethics, external relations, communications, and strategic planning for a wide range of public and private sector clients in the United States and abroad. Linsky is a graduate of Williams College and Harvard Law School. He has been a journalist, a lawyer, and a politician, having served as a Member and Assistant Minority Leader of the Massachusetts House of Representatives. His most recent book is a coauthorship with Dr. Ronald Heifetz entitled *Leadership on the Line: Staying Alive through the Dangers of Leading* (Harvard Business School Press, 2002). He lives in New York City with his wife, Lynn Staley, Assistant Managing Editor (Design) of *Newsweek* magazine. He has three children: Alison, Sam, and Max.

ANNIE MCKEE is co-Chair of the Teleos Leadership Institute, where her work focuses on leadership and strategic planning initiatives at Fortune 100 firms as well as leadership/community development projects for developing countries all over the world. She also serves on the faculty of the University of Pennsylvania, teaches at the Wharton School's Aresty Institute of Executive Education, and is the former Director of Management Development Services for Hay Group. Most recently, in collaboration with Daniel Goleman and Richard

Boyatzis, she has completed a book entitled *Primal Leadership: Realizing the Power of Emotional Intelligence* (Harvard Business School Press, 2002). Dr. McKee received her baccalaureate degree from Chaminade University of Honolulu and her doctorate in Organizational Behavior from Case Western Reserve Univer-sity. She lives in Elkins Park, Pennsylvania, with her husband and three children.

MARYANNE PEABODY is Cofounder and Vice President of Stybel Peabody Lincolnshire. Since 1981 she has consulted with executives and professionals making career and job transitions. Prior to founding the firm, Peabody held various management positions in the health care industry. Peabody received her M.B.A. from Southern Methodist University in Dallas, where she was the first recipient of the Hoblitzelle Foundation's Women in Business Scholarship.

LAURENCE J. STYBEL, ED.D., is Cofounder of Stybel Peabody Lincolnshire, a Boston-based firm. Founded in 1979, Stybel Peabody Lincolnshire helps companies manage the senior executive assignment cycle. Its retained search practice is limited to positions touching the Board. Its coaching focuses on providing a board perspective for senior executives and better managing the Board/CEO axis. He obtained his doctorate in organization behavior at Harvard University under Chris Argyris. He previously worked as an executive compensation consultant for Hay Associates.

Index

197